KW-240-024

Reconstituting Sovereignty

Post-Dayton Bosnia uncovered

RORY KEANE
Civic Education Project, Belgrade Open School, Yugoslavia

Ashgate

© Rory Keane 2002

All rights reserved. No part of this publication may be reproduced, stored in a retrieval system or transmitted in any form or by any means, electronic, mechanical, photocopying, recording or otherwise without the prior permission of the publisher.

The author has asserted his moral right under the Copyright, Designs and Patents Act, 1988, to be identified as the author of this work.

Published by
Ashgate Publishing Limited
Gower House
Croft Road
Aldershot
Hampshire GU11 3HR
England

Ashgate Publishing Company
131 Main Street
Burlington, VT 05401-5600 USA

Ashgate website: http://www.ashgate.com

British Library Cataloguing in Publication Data
Keane, Rory
  Reconstituting sovereignty : post-Dayton Bosnia uncovered.
  - (The international political economy of new regionalisms)
  1.Conflict management - Bosnia and Hercegovina
  2.Nationalism - Bosnia and Hercegovina 3.Sovereignty
  4.International relations 5.Bosnia and Hercegovina -
  Politics and government - 1992-
  I.Title
  327.1'7'0949742

Library of Congress Control Number: 2001096471

ISBN 0 7546 1859 5

Printed and bound in Great Britain by Antony Rowe Ltd, Chippenham, Wiltshire

Dedicated to my parents

UNIVERSITY OF PLYMOUTH

Item No.	9005086012
Date	2 3 MAY 2002 Z
Class No.	327.49742 KEA
Cont. No.	✓

PLYMOUTH LIBRARY

Contents

Preface

Too often of late has the death of the nation state been preempted. In reality, however, nationalism remains on the rise. Today in the Balkans, regions such as Tetovo, the Sandjak and Mostar remain engulfed in insecurity deriving from the paradigm of nationalism. Heralding the death of the nation state in an academic sense is all very well, replacing it with a unit of governance more in tune with human security is much the greater task. In writing this book, the will to human security conditioned my thought process. Today International Relations as a discipline appears lost. International Relations theory may be beginning to depart from theories, which simply explain the world, but we appear reluctant to create what has not already existed, we lack the imaginative ability to deconstruct in line with need. In essence we destroy ambiguity in the will to clarity. Within this largely theoretical work I celebrate deconstruction in line with need, I accepted the ambiguities that must exist in a world of complexity. I set the agenda of International Relations upon its ability to change the world in line with human security.

Broadly speaking books written on International Relations divide into theoretical and practical works. I promised myself to attempt to bridge such a divide in the writing of this work, as theory without practical application, to put it simply, is too easy. Practical works, however, can too easily become the stuff of *real-politik.* This book critiques the potential ability and extent to which both post-Dayton Bosnia may be able to provide new and more responsive forms of governance. The case of Bosnia and Herzegovina is interesting insofar as it manifests firstly how nationalism acts as the antithesis to human security. Secondly, the *Dayton Peace Accord* which brought the war to an end in 1995 warrants research insofar as it creates new forms of institutional framework which mark a departure from the traditional sovereign nation state structure. The architects of Dayton (including Richard Holbrooke), the ethno-nationalist political parties in Bosnia and indeed the International community charged with implementing Dayton, did and still do have as their aim the creation of a archetype-Westphalian nation state.

To date they have failed in that aim, and rather post-Dayton implementation reflects partially functioning sovereign constructs which may serve in time to form the basis of post-nation state governance. Ironically, in this sense, the failure of Dayton to create a nation state has left it potentially more able to respond to the socio-political habitat in Bosnia and Herzegovina.

This book divides into seven chapters. The first two chapters are largely theoretical. I firstly outline what I consider to be the basis of human security. Thereafter I introduce a theoretical model, based upon the reconstitution of sovereignty. Chapter three breaks into two sections and utilizes a genealogical approach so as to uproot the unnaturalness in pursuing a nation state model as a means to human security in the Balkans. Chapters four to seven concentrate upon the *Dayton Peace Accord*, Dayton implementation and the extent to which Dayton implementation signposts a certain deconstruction of nation state sovereignty. It is evident from this work, that Dayton implementation has prevented the spillover of ethno-nationalism in Bosnia and therefore has prevented another fratricidal ethnic conflict. Neither has the institutional framework created human security however, due to the power of nationalism. Within chapter five the principal practical issues which hold the ability to weaken the strength of nationalism in Bosnia are documented. Chapter six shows that steady, although slow, progress has been made towards creating a more inclusive and somewhat less nationalist Bosnia, based upon the unbundling of sovereignty.

This book is based broadly upon my PhD. Much of the content has also been presented at international conferences in Belgrade, Tehran, Columbia University and Quebec. This work was made possible by the unyielding support and friendship of my PhD supervisor, Dr. Lucian M. Ashworth (University of Limerick). I also wish to thank Dr. Mark Downes (West University Timisaoura), John A. Loonam and Jack Anderson (University of Limerick). In addition, the Department of Government and Society, University of Limerick has always been supportive financially and otherwise. I also wish to thank my current employers, the Civic Education Project (CEP) and the Belgrade Open School for affording me the time to complete this work. Finally, I wish to thank Orla Sheehy for being Orla Sheehy.

List of Abbreviations

BiH	Bosnia and Herzegovina
DPA	Dayton Peace Accord
DP	Displaced Person
ECHO	European Community Humanitarian Office
ECMM	European Community Monitoring Mission
GFAP	General Framework Agreement for Peace
HDZ	Croatian Democratic Union (Croat)
HVO	Croat Council of Defense
IEBL	Inter-Entity Boundary Line
IFOR	NATO led implementation force
IPTF	International Police Task Force
JNA	Yugoslav Peoples' Army
LCY	The Communist League of Yugoslavia
NDH	Independent State of Croatia (1941)
OHR	Office of the High Representative
OSCE	Organisation for Security and Co-operation in Europe
PDP	Party of Democratic Progress
PEC	Provisional Election Commission
RRTF	Reconstruction and return task force
RS	Republika Srpska
SBiH	Party for Bosnia and Herzegovina
SDA	Party for Democratic Action (Bosniak)
SDP	Social Democratic Party (Bosniak)
SDS	Serbian Democratic Party (Serb)
SFOR	NATO led stabilisation force that succeeded IFOR
SMP	The Union for Peace and Progress
SNSD	Party of Independent Social Democrats
SRS	Serbian Radical Party
UNPROFOR	United Nations Protection Force

Chapter 1
Human Security and International Relations

The fact that French toys literally prefigure the world of adult functions obviously cannot but prepare the child to accept them all, by constituting for him, even before he can think about it, the alibi of a Nature which has at all times created soldiers, postmen and Vespas. Toys here reveal the list of all the things the adult does not find unusual: war, bureaucracy, ugliness, Martians, etc... However, faced with this world of faithful and complicated objects, the child can only identify himself as owner, as user, never as creator; he does not invent the world, he uses it: there are, prepared for him, actions without adventure, without wonder, without joy.[1]

Citizens of the world today can indeed be equated to the French child, as the overarching toy of modernity, namely the nation state, prefigures the world for us. In this sense we can only ever identify ourselves as owner, as user, never as creator, as we have not created the nation state as the unit of social organisation. We live in nation states, we belong to nation states, but we never decide upon it as the unit of social organisation.

On the odd occasion, the French child is allowed to use a set of blocks. A set of blocks implies a very different understanding of the world; as the blocks allow the child to create the world. "The actions he performs are not those of a user but those of a demiurge. He creates forms which walk, which roll, he creates life, not property: objects now act as themselves, they are no longer an inert and complicated material in the palm of his hand."[2] When the citizens of the world find human emancipation, which allows the creation of a world in line with needs, duties, desire and impression, we will be in a position to mould a more amiable existence for humankind.

It is my aim to deliver a means to human emancipation, by fulfilling need, duty and desire. In this respect the causes of insecurity must be deciphered, challenged and replaced with a sense of human security or ontological security.[3]

Emancipation can only be achieved by broadening the discourse of security so as to include human solidarity.[4] As outlined by Barry Buzan in *People, States and Fear* the discourse of security has been underdeveloped and largely confined to empirical definition and realist understanding.[5] In broadening the definition of security, I focus upon human security as a means of delivering human emancipation. Human security is based upon the complex fusion between *Innenwelt* and *Umwelt*,[6] between agent and structure.[7] Emancipation can only be achieved when the needs of the individual (agent) are reconciled with that of the world (structure). Political and social theorists down through the ages, from Hobbes and Locke to Henri Saint Simon, have attempted to find compromise between the needs of *Innenwelt* and *Umwelt*. I do not aim to create a social contract between the two binaries, based upon compromise. Rather the aim of this book is to *reconcile* the binary opposition between agent and structure. Defining security as the reconciliation between agent and structure allows for the creation of human emancipation based upon a fusion between "us" and "them".

A Challenge to the Primacy of the Nation State

In instilling reconciliation between "us" and "them", I develop upon an argument forwarded by Richard Rorty, which puts a strong emphasis upon our duty and responsibility to *create* human solidarity, as opposed to mere Kantian moral obligation. "In my utopia, human solidarity would be seen not as a fact to be recognised by clearing away "prejudice" or burrowing down to previously hidden depths but, rather, as a goal to be achieved. It is to be achieved not by inquiry but by imagination, the imaginative ability to see strange people as fellow suffers. Solidarity is not discovered by reflection but created."[8]

Within International Relations today the principal cause of human insecurity stems from intra-state conflict. It is the aim of this book to show how intra-state insecurity can be eradicated, through a reinterpretation of International Relations theory. In achieving this aim it is necessary to reduce the primacy of the nation state as the overriding unit of analysis within IR. This area of research is underdeveloped and until recently has been largely ignored, particularly within the realist school. Realist scholars have rather accepted the nation state as a "natural", "essential" and "timeless" feature of human existence. It is a primary purpose of this work to falsify the "naturalness" of the nation state. By the very fact that the character of the nation state is so tightly interrelated with complex phenomena such as sovereignty and nationalism, it can be difficult to see how the phenomenon of the nation state can be by-passed. Recently, however, a number of theorists have come to question the nation state, showing it to be a human construction and a distinctly modern form. Benedict Anderson's celebrated work *Imagined Communities* elaborates upon this theme in a most convincing fashion.[9] Within this work he explicitly makes the point that what was "imagined" and recently created may be "unimagined" and subsequently demolished. To date, however, such re-imagining or reconfiguration of the state has failed to by-pass the very inhibiting contours of the nation state apparatus, namely, territoriality, nationalism and sovereignty. Although postmodern International Relations theory may be wishing away the nation state, the power of nationalism appears as strong as ever. We may be witnessing a growth in supra and sub national constructions, however, many of these institutions are impeded by a reverence to territoriality and nation state sovereignty. "The only real change is a change of geographical scale."[10] In forwarding an avenue towards deconstructing the nation state, this work presents theoretical qualitative challenges to the state structure. The aim is to disaggregate power from the centre and simultaneously emancipate and (de)alienate peoples. Such an approach is vital at this stage in human development, as reverent adherence to the nation state no longer presents solutions to conflict, which are increasingly fought on the basis of nationalism (articulated through religion, ethnicity, culture etc.). Solutions to such conflict cannot be found in the nation state, as the duress of the nation state is very much the cause of contemporary conflict. By definition nationalist movements struggling to achieve nation state status inadvertently maintain the principal of nation state sovereignty. By attempting to legitimise their cause through nation state criteria, namely, religion, culture, ethnicity, etc., nationalist movements implicitly strengthen a nation state's awareness and sense of "self". An acceptance of the nation state as the unit of analysis thus fails to present an escape route from the quagmire of nationalist conflict. Within this work a theoretical avenue is constructed capable of circumventing the quagmire of nationalist conflict. This theoretical "escape route" is achieved by challenging the modern definition of state sovereignty. In redefining the character of sovereignty, a dis-aggregation or "unbundling"[11] of territoriality from sovereignty is undertaken. In aiming to dis-aggregate territoriality from sovereignty my work is clearly influenced and responsive to Mitranian functionalism, which promotes the decoupling of nation from state.[12]

The Ubiquitous Nature of Rationalism within IR

Within the discipline of International Relations rationality dictates our understanding and conception of human behaviour, international conflict, anarchy and indeed every area of life. The criticism of this rational approach, which prevails over the discipline of International Relations, is that it leads and directs our understanding from a certain perspective. Through rationalism we come to accept specific structures or procedures as axiomatic, ontological, pathological etc. The ubiquitous nature of the rational approach is most identifiable within realist and neo-realist theoretical approaches. Kenneth N. Waltz work *Man the State and War* is a prime example of this approach. Operating from Rousseau's perspective, Waltz accepts that man is naturally neither good nor bad, but that it is the polity or the society in which he lives that makes him good or bad. Waltz expresses this view as "the first image". According to this image the evilness of men, or their improper behaviour, leads to war; individual goodness, if it could be universalised on the other hand, would mean peace. However, regarding the first image, Waltz appears reluctant to become embroiled in a futile debate on the essence of human nature. Within the second image, Waltz looks at the state as a means by which war can be both curtailed and created. In simple terms the state is both envisaged as a protector and as the cause of conflict and war, good states protect their citizens while bad states exploit their citizens. According to the third image, there is a constant possibility of war in a world in which there are two or more states each seeking to promote a set of interests and having no agency above them that they can rely for protection.[13] It is not wholly necessary to recount Waltz's three images in detail, what is significant, however, is the fact that both the second image and particularly the third image, which Waltz puts great credence upon, are seen as both logical and rational.[14] In both images the cause of conflict is identified in terms of which all other causes of conflict are to be understood. In this sense, Waltz identifies International Relations as a conflict between the three rational, all encompassing absolutes within modernity, namely, man, the state and the international. He then proceeds to analyse the conflict prone interaction between the rational absolutes, before prescribing well-rounded timeless recommendations.

Rationality has thus permeated International Relations theory in the most ubiquitous manner since the Enlightenment. Axiomatic principles, such as the nation state and nationalism, enshrined by the rational mind of modernity, are seriously called into question within the chapters that follow. Over the past number of years the rational approach, which holds the relationship between state and society as axiomatic has come to experience fundamental theoretical challenges. The whole essence of rationality, which is based upon clear and distinct ideas of progress, linearity, spatiality and positivistic deduction, is now open to question. All that was solid is beginning to melt and, therefore, shared sensory reality is seen as an illusion. The ethos of rationality, so well orchestrated by theorists such as John Locke, now finds itself vulnerable. Locke, working from a rational mindset, believed that the proper starting point to be found resides in "shared sensory evidence" or ideas of sense. What Locke, as a quintessential rationalist, failed to comprehend was that ideas of sense were firstly open to interpretation and secondly could possibly rest upon false assumptions. Thus, there can be no pure rationality. In *The Second Treatise of Government*, Locke develops a critique of society based upon this idea of sense. For example, Locke maintains that there are certain inalienable rights; he also states that the powers of governments are based entirely on powers transferred to them by individuals. Again Locke maintains that the state of nature is not necessarily a state of war of all against all.[15] All such principles, as admirable as they might be, are based upon an idea of sense, an idea of rationality, just as the modern nation state is considered both rational and reasonable. In opening Lockean rationality to question, rational structures such as the nation state are also open to interrogation.

Creating Multiple Identity Representation

In aiming to circumnavigate the nation state, and thereby circumvent the primary source of binary opposition, a theoretical formula capable of representing multiple identities is constructed. This process involves the development of a form of dispersed vertical and horizontal sovereignty, which is explained in chapter two. With the deconstruction of the sovereign nation state and the reconstruction of dispersed vertical and horizontal sovereignty, I theoretically begin to channel a route capable of circumnavigating the nation state and threatening communitarian nationalism, which traditionally has served as a dichotomising agent and thus an instigator of human insecurity. Such a formulation can help solidify the development of *human security*, if one terms *human security* as the tangible emancipation of identities. This can be achieved through both dispersed vertical sovereignty, which aims to give a voice to all identities, and horizontal sovereignty, which aims to tangibly support the needs of all identities.

The clear evidence of inhumanity and brutality stemming from recent conflict (Rwanda, Bosnia, Kosovo, Kurdistan) deserves a clear and convincing response from the international world. Yet the deafening silence and inaction from the international world signals clearly that the approach of *real politik* is unable or perhaps unwilling to deal with such complex intra-state warfare. For example, it appeared thus that the ethicopolitical dilemma that was the Balkans had surpassed the intellectual capacity of traditional International Relations theory. "The moral cartography of the Cold War was sustained by, and in turn nourished, the hegemony of realist perspectives in the discipline."[16] Following the Cold War realist and indeed neo-realist theory could no longer adequately explain the world in which we lived. The wars in the Balkans vividly displayed that a deeper ground breaking theoretical approach was necessary to help solve such post Cold War conflicts. The character of the vast majority of post Cold War conflicts erupted clearly as a result of ethnic and nationalist passions. Lasting solutions to such conflicts can only be found through a rethinking and reappraisal of theoretical approaches. Traditional IR approaches with their foundations rooted clearly in the sovereign nation state can no longer be theoretically considered sufficient for the purpose of solving such conflicts.

Deconstructing the State Structure

A deconstruction of the state appears to open the door to possible solutions in this post Cold War period. When one considers that within the former Yugoslavia the cause of conflict is based solely upon the concept of state alignment or consolidation, it becomes clear that a deconstruction of the state rather than a strengthening of the state structure is the answer. A process of deconstruction may be instilled, in a practical sense, through the development of functional institutions, based upon human need and duty.

In this regard, the deconstruction of the nation state might allow for the gradual transfer of sovereignty to functional institutions, according to social needs and political developments. If we persist with futile state based solutions, we invariably, enshrine the sentiment articulated by the deputy commander of Bosnian Serb nationalist forces, General Milan Gvero, "We say everybody has to live on his own territory, Muslims on Muslim territory, Serbs on Serbian... This (Serb areas in Bosnia) is pure Serbian territory, and there is no power on earth that can make us surrender it".[17]

Such sentiment, by correlating ethnicity with territory, could only ignite conflict in a multi-ethnic society such as Bosnia. Deconstruction is the only means of eroding the exclusionary dichotomy of identity versus difference. Working from this premise clearly places this work within the theoretical realm of critical International Relations theory.

New insecurities are not about defending disputed boundaries, power rivalries, or security dilemmas between states, as was the case in the Cold War era. Instead, today issues of identity and migration are driving underlying perceptions of threats and vulnerabilities. In the chapters that follow the insecurities which drive conflict are challenged fundamentally in a theoretical and practical sense. I intend to theoretically develop the means by which such growing insecurities can be limited through a rereading of International Relations from a critical perspective. In a practical sense, I wish to assess the extent to which the implementation of the *Dayton Peace Accord* reflects the theoretical approach developed. I focus upon *Dayton Peace Accord* implementation for two predominant reasons. Firstly, the *Accord* itself codified a form of sovereign dispersal whish is unorthodox within International Relations. Secondly, it remains a fundamental question, whether sovereign dispersal can in fact allow the creation and celebration of multiple identity membership, so necessary in a multi-ethnic society such as Bosnia.

Punctuations: the Graph of IR Theory

International Relations theory for the purpose of comprehension is often sectionalised into three great debates. These three great debates are regarded as capturing key tensions in what are understood to be the general theoretical principles guiding research in the discipline. The idea of three great debates is, however, both a lazy and unhelpful narrative, insofar as the debates never occurred. In fact, contrary to the idea of debate, theoretical schools within IR have tended to ignore each other and have generally failed to incorporate elements of other theories. In mapping the contours of IR theory if may be more useful and accurate to speak of punctuations on the graph of IR theory. The first punctuations saw the development of idealist and realist theories and hinges on the first and second world wars as reference points. The prominence of both idealism and realism in the twentieth century resulted in more critical approaches being marginalised.

Methodologically, both the dominance of positivism in the post-World War Two environment and the rise of behavouralism from the 1960s onwards can be considered as significant methodological punctuations. Within recent years there has been a convergence between quantitative and qualitative (positivist and behavoiuralist) sociological methods within social science. It would appear both logical and rational that IR theory should follow the same path, especially considering that the basic principles of both are similar and that it is in essence really only methodology that separates them.

Recent punctuations in the discipline of IR have been both epistemological and methodological in nature. One of the most significant developments, which strongly influenced the critical school of IR, has been the identification of theory as discourse. To accept this hypothesis is to accept that theory is an important variable in the manufacture of power, ideology and culture. "It requires an awareness of the degree to which theoretical discourse is embedded in social practices more generally. Similar to all practices, it takes place in time and space, and draws together associations from past and present that link time and space in particular ways."[18] In becoming conscious of the power of theory in fashioning conceptions, theorists can begin to take into account the function of power and knowledge and thereafter begin to question perceived truths. What we are beginning to see in essence is a major paradigm shift in IR as a response to the increasing use and relevance of post-positivist approaches.

Ken Booth and the Major Paradigm Shift within IR

Ken Booth attempts to broaden the focus of International Relations theory. Booth went through a process of intellectual metamorphoses, finally rejecting the realist outlook and thereafter attempting to push the parameters of realism and in so doing has opened up new and useful debates within International Relations. In this respect he represents a liaison between the realist and critical school of thought, between the first and third punctuation. Rather than following the threadbare route taken by realist/idealist theorists who merely turn all theoretical arguments into a Hobbes versus Kant banter. Booth is concerned with questioning, criticising and confronting existing theory. In this regard he is prepared to challenge the axiomatic rationalism and doctrine of utilisation, which has inhibited all traditional International Relations theory.

This challenge to the axiomatic is most vividly displayed in a 1994 paper, "Security and Self Reflections of a Fallen Realist".[19] Here he questions his own realist mindset, and in so doing attempts to develop a broader more interpretative account of International Relations. "Instead of purporting to describe or explain the world "out there", as is one's professional training. I want to reflect upon the world "in here" as part of our innermost being."[20] Here we see the development of a more self-reflective Booth. In outlining this self-reflective process he concentrates specifically upon the concept of security, which is central to a realist understanding of world order. Rather than delving into the shortcomings of realist security concerns, he instead attempts to reconceptulise the meaning of security; in this respect he makes reference to Mead. "According to Mead, the human self is a reflective being made up of an *I* and a *me*."[21] Booth has come to realise that society has socially constructed his *self*, namely the *me*, as a realist. It appears he has come to realise that he indeed is a victim/construction of the Cold War, insofar as his philosophies were conditioned by the Cold War. Booth therefore sets about reflecting upon himself as "the I".

More innately he has been victimised by the doctrine of utilisation and rationalisation. He therefore attempts to break away from the realist mindset and in *New Thinking about Strategy and International Security*[22] he details his broadening definition of security. Here Booth draws upon the significant point that national security perspectives are grounded within the realms of self-interest. This fact, in addition to manifesting the significance of Hobbesian philosophy in today's world, also shows itself to be antithetical to any form of global interdependence. Obviously interdependence can only operate in a most cumbersome manner in relation to a system that is inherently based upon self-interest. The question that must be posed, however, is to what extent the "self" can feel secure within such a disjointed system. Ironically self-interest demands military, political and ever increasing economic security so as to safeguard the "self" from the "other". Of course the perpetuating conundrum arises as each "self" in making itself secure invariable increases the insecurity of the "other". Indeed there is nothing at all new in such a dichotomy between "self" and "other", as it merely represents the simple dualism incorporated within all modern western philosophy and indeed all-traditional IR theory. Booth to his credit attempts to analyse to what extent the growing military, economic and political interdependence helps bridge the dualism of "self" versus "other" inherent in all critiques of modern security discourse. He is less inclined to agree with Buzan's account of mature anarchy or Keohane and Nye's account of economic interdependence, as resulting in greater co-operation. On the contrary, "interdependence is unlikely to reduce conflict and may increase it by giving states a broader agenda of issues over which their interests and circumstances will differ".[23] On a more optimistic note he also records the fact that it is more and more in the "self interest" of states, in the age of global interdependence, to restrain from certain types of conflict including nuclear, economic and ecological conflict. It appears therefore that "common interests" pertain to such issues. Booth is optimistic regarding this point and envisages international security as being "located within the complex dialectic that results from the dividing tendencies of anarchy interacting with the binding ones of interdependence".[24]

It must be remembered however that this complex dialectic can only operate in a partial manner. What I mean by this is that it can only occur where there is sufficient common interest to hold all parties together. From this standpoint it is difficult to see how the concept of common security, as articulated by Booth, surpasses the doctrine of utilisation and rationalisation that has prevailed in all modern strains of western political philosophy. Is he not simply stating that common security may and indeed does provide a number of footbridges between the "self" and "other", thus reducing anarchy and developing greater security? To what extent the realms of common security can broaden to encompass more sensitive areas is however questionable, considering that common security today functions on mere pragmatic "self interest" grounds, as the self interest of specific states collides fortuitously with the self interest of other states. Common security has thus done little in eradicating the dualism of "self" and "other" and thus cannot deliver human security.

Booth's Emphasis upon Emancipation as Security   Booth does, however, set his sights upon creating "human emancipation" as a distinct objective. In using the term human emancipation he is purporting to the aim of community building in a bid to break down the barriers between "us" and "them". In manifesting the soundness of this argument he points to the work of political leaders such as Brendt, Genscher and Gorbachev. According to Booth true security will follow when human emancipation has been achieved. Richard Rummel's work supports such an argument. "He argues that there is an inverse correlation between the political rights and civil liberties in nations and both internal violence and war."[25] In other words emancipation and security are interchangeable, as they are in fact the same thing. Emancipation is thus closely related to security, the security of the individual against war, poverty, poor education and political oppression. "Emancipation theoretically is security."[26] It appears therefore that traditional security has missed the point altogether in its concentration upon "objects" (states, territory, geopolitics, military, strategy etc.) at the expense of "subjects" (individual humans beings). This security dichotomy with emphasises upon power and order as opposed to the citizens of the world has accentuated human insecurity worldwide. Perhaps if International Relations theorists had responded positively to the words of Hedley Bull in *the Anarchical Society*, which pertain to the emancipation of humanity, "...the ultimate units of the great society of all mankind are not states but individual human beings",[27] the great dichotomy which has perpetuated insecurity within modernity would by now have been laid to rest. The concept of security incorporating human emancipation is however void in relation to the dominant stream of IR theory. This is most vividly displayed in the metaphors and images utilised within IR theoretical discourse. For example, as stated by Paul A. Chilton, "the container image lies at the heart of western political discourse".[28] This container image as a means of explaining security is of powerful significance. The image constitutes an understanding of inside and outside. Inside represents the nation state, national allegiance etc. whilst outside represents the competitive world. This dualism between inside and outside has done little, except intensify insecurities and confine the emancipation of individual humans. Inside becomes associated with government, legality and freedom of action, while outside represents an anarchical world where actions are determined by self-interest and human nature.

Working Outside the Dualism of the Container Image

Simon Dalby has attempted to erode this dualism or container-like structure which has inhibited a broadening definition of security. In this regard he attempts to develop human emancipation, firstly by defining the global security *problematique* and secondly by broadening its agenda. He strikes a note with Booth in his realisation that security to date has concentrated more on power and order rather than on the insecurities pertaining to ordinary people. "...[S]ecurity is defined in spatial terms of exclusion; enemies are created as Others, inhabiting some other territory."[29] Therefore identity is still privileged over difference, creating an ordered dualism whereby our security is dependent upon both exclusion and preponderance over outsiders. Dalby firstly attempts to emancipate the individual from insecurity by broadening the scope or agenda of security. He comes to fundamentally question "how a particular series of "security discourses" establishes an ideological space from which to dominate, exclude and delegitimize other discourses…".[30]

Dalby opens up a multiplicity of other worlds by including societal phenomena as integral to security concerns. For example, he critiques the global economic interdependence encompassing the world today. He maintains that although global interdependence should indeed ensure "our" prosperity, the southern states or more specifically the people of the southern states will continue to experience ever increasing deprivation. He also adds environmental security to his broadening definition of security, articulating the ironic fact that, "security understood as the perpetuation of the modern order seems antithetical to the preservation of the environment".[31] Again a vivid demarcation between neo-realist and critical theory can be located. For example, whereas Buzan envisages "mature anarchy" deriving from global interdependence and complex military alliances, Dalby can only see social injustice and ecological destruction.

Them versus Us

R.B.J. Walker and David Campbell point to the "splinter like" effect of state sovereignty and foreign policy respectively upon security and more specifically insecurity. R.B.J. Walker tackles the ethos of dichotomy enshrined within modernity, which perpetuates a sense of insecurity. State sovereignty in particular creates and instigates such dichotomy between inside and outside. According to Walker, it appears that most IR theorists have come to accept answers to questions about the kind of world that we are trying to know. The predominant reason, according to Walker, which reframes all theory from delving outside the accepted rational theoretical model, arises from the dominant historical understanding encompassed within modernity, which has stunted innovative theoretical interpretation. So much so that, "theorists of international relations are easily drawn into an affirmation of them as a convenient myth of origins".[32] This predominant account of western macro history gives priority to the Enlightenment, entailing progressive emancipation and the emergence of modern conceptions of freedom, justice and rationality.

International architecture and institutions within the school of International Relations have grown and developed from this particular historical analysis of modernity. Walker detests this approach and instead promotes sensitivity to history and time, so obviously void from traditional accounts of IR theory. In "Security, Sovereignty, and the Challenge of

World Politics" Walker attempts to overcome certain limits in the way we have been able to think about more desirable alternatives to our restricted historical account of security. In meshing the theme of state sovereignty with that of security Walker opens up many new channels of analysis, which challenge our traditional historical beliefs regarding the state, sovereignty and security. According to Walker our simple straightforward account of security is fashioned by its close relationship with the principle of state sovereignty, a principle that in fact has accentuated and indeed perpetuated fragmentation and thus accentuated and perpetuated insecurities. Yet ironically state sovereignty, "is treated as the primary "fact" of international relations".[33] State sovereignty has also served in accentuating the dichotomy between "inside" and "outside". "Within states it is assumed to be possible to pursue justice and virtue, to aspire to universal standards of reason. Outside, however, there are merely relations."[34] This presents a basic contradiction within world politics, namely that there is invariable a conflict between universality and particularity, space and time, them and us etc. Can human security ever be maintained within the sharp division of inclusion and exclusion? Sadly the answer is no, as entrenched nationalism, ecological disaster, economic exploitation and nuclear balance of terror explicitly manifest. David Campbell again augments the visibility of this great dichotomy between "us" and "them" utilising the example of the ever-expanding field of state foreign policy.[35] Unlike Rosenau's ideal where foreign policy is considered as a "bridging discipline" linking "us" and "them", Campbell maintains that foreign policy helps maintain the territorial state. Foreign policy is thus a trajectory of state sovereignty and nationalism all of which legitimise the power of the state, and all of which are perpetuated by a sense of danger. Each state thus, in protecting itself from danger and thus legitimising its existence launches specific foreign policy procedures. This process is perpetual, as danger "out there" is constantly in a state of flux: as the Cold War recedes, Islamic fundamentalism intensifies.

The Nation State – the Underlying Cause of Dichotomy

It is time to challenge the underlying cause of such dichotomies within International Relations, namely the nation state. The state thus appears to be the unquestioned given which has dichotomised International Relations and subsequently perpetuated human insecurity. The transcendence of the dominant unquestioned theoretical model utilises a specific reading of history so as to validate its origins and transgression. The dominant reading of history, with its emphasis upon *spatio-temporality*, has seen it necessary to promote state sovereignty, so as to prevent anarchy and chaos attributed to the flux of temporality. In this regard, state sovereignty may regulate and territorially delineate spatial co-ordinates, thus preventing chaos in times of great temporal flux. Modernity has utilised the Treaties of Westphalia (1648) and the Enlightenment to carve out such an understanding. The preponderant ethos of modernity has endeavoured to perpetuate its philosophy ever since, utilising the tools of rationality, reality, objectivity and positivism so as to promote the necessity of sovereignty, nationalism, realist foreign policy etc. Critical theoretical discourse has thus been stunted within the confines of epistemology and its principal tool of investigation-positivism. This has been achieved mainly insofar as epistemology was and is considered hierarchically superior over ontology, hermeneutics, axiology etc.

In the words of James Rosenau, "we do not know how to be puzzled, how to tolerate ambiguity for a while, how to suspend interpretations until after we have experienced awe in the regularity of recurrent patterns or the challenge of singular anomalies".[36] Critical theory appears, at least to some extent, to have risen to the challenge outlined by Rosenau. One may interpret George's work "Realist Ethics, International Relations and Post Modernism" as incorporating the "puzzlement" aspired to by Rosenau. Rather than aspiring to the idealised realm of universal ethical truth, International Relations should be both self reflective and assume a critical awareness, in analysing history, culture, politics and linguistics, according to George. Within this work, I assume critical awareness regarding what is perceived to be the axiomatic relationship between sovereignty and territory. A high level of ambiguity and complexity is also accepted throughout. In this sense, the theoretical model developed remains both adaptable and open to interpretation. In addition it remains "unclear" whether the *Dayton Peace Accord* can in itself reside conformably inside the theoretical model. It is simply argued that the *Dayton Peace Accord* possesses elements of the theoretical model, and therefore warrants research.

Notes

[1] Barthes, Roland, *Mythologies* (London: Jonathan Cape Ltd., 1972), pp. 53-54.

[2] Ibid.

[3] "Ontological security relates to the self, its social competence, its confidence in the actor's capacity to manage relations with others. It is a security of social relationship, a sense of being safely in cognitive control of the interaction context. It is relational at the most basic level of interaction: that of the mutual knowledge which is a condition of action, and which derives from a sense of shared community." See McSweeney, Bill, *Security, Identity and Interests, A Sociology of International Relations* (Cambridge: Cambridge University Press, 1999), p. 157.

[4] David Campbell expands the discourse of security away from realist nationalist security issues in his acclaimed work, *Writing Security-US Foreign policy and the Politics of Identity*. See Campbell, David, *Writing Security-US Foreign Policy and the Politics of Identity* (Manchester: Manchester University Press, 1992).

[5] See Buzan, Barry, *People, States and Fear* (New York: Harvester Wheatsheaf, 1991), pp. 7-11.

[6] Lacan uses the terms *Innenwelt* and *Umwelt* to explain the relationship between an organism (Innenwelt) and its reality (Umwelt). See Lacan, Jacques, *Ecrits: a selection* (translated by Alan Sheridan, New York: W.W. Norton and Company, 1977), p. 4.

[7] Anthony Giddens defines the symbiotic relationship between agent (people) and structure (the world). "There is a continuous interaction between agent and structure(s). Simply put: agents make society and society makes people – the process is dual, continuous and codetermined." See Giddens, Anthony, in: Baaz, Mikael (2000) "Meta-Theoretical Foundations for the Study of Global Social Relations from the Perspective of the New Political Economy of Development", *Journal of International Relations and Development* Vol. 2, No. 4, p. 463.

[8] See Rorty, Richard, *Contingency, Irony and Change* (Cambridge: Cambridge University Press, 1989), p. xvi.

[9] Anderson, Benedict, *Imagined Communities: reflections on the origins and spread of nationalism* (London: Verso, 1983). Other relevant works include, Kearney, Richard, *Post-nationalist Ireland: politics, literature, philosophy* (New York: Routledge, 1996); Ruggie, J.G. (1993) "Territoriality and beyond: problematizing modernity in *International Relations as* international relations", *International Organization*, Vol. 47, No. 1, pp. 139-74; Walker, R.B.J., *Inside/Outside: Political Theory* (Cambridge: Cambridge University Press, 1993).

[10] Anderson, James, *et al*, *A Global World* (Oxford: The Open University, 1995), p. 72. Supra and sub national structures fail to deconstruct the classical homogeneous conception of space, as geographical size is the only real change occurring. Rather the so-called "theme of Gulliver" prevails where Littiput resembles our human world in everything but its smaller size; Brobdingnag likewise is merely bigger. See Walker, R.B.J., Op cit., p. 133.

[11] John Gerard Ruggie developed this term; see Ruggie, J.G., Op cit., p. 159.

[12] Mitranian functionalism, in aiming to overcome the sovereign power of the nation state by constructing appropriate structures that are not territorially based, but instead based upon a need or duty, has clearly different emphasis than Parsonian functionalism. Rather Parson's "... saw society as a functioning whole, and was concerned with how the social order was maintained, and how various institutions in society function to contribute to this

maintenance". See Marsh, Ian (ed.), *Sociology: Making sense of society* (Essex: Pearson Education Limited, 2000), p. 441.

[13] Waltz, Kenneth N., *Man the State and War* (New York: Columbia University Press, 1954).

[14] The same rational logic cannot be applied to the first image, as the image is based upon the essence of human nature, which can neither be proven nor defined.

[15] Locke, John, *Political Writings* (Harmondsworth: Penguin Books, 1993).

[16] Campbell, David, in: Lapid and Kratochwil (eds.), *The Return of Culture and Identity in IR Theory* (London: Lynne Rienner Publishers, 1996), p. 164.

[17] Quoted in *New York Times*, "Exuding Confidence, Serbian Nationalists Act as if War for Bosnia is Won", May 23, 1993, p. 12.

[18] Youngs, Gillian, *International Relations in a Global Age* (Cambridge: Polity Press, 1999), p. 59.

[19] Booth, Ken (1994), "Security and Reflections of a Fallen Realist" Toronto: *YCISS Occasional paper*, number 26.

[20] Berger, 1996, in: ibid., p. 1.

[21] Mead, 1934, in: ibid., p. 5.

[22] Very useful regarding Booth's broadening definition of security and security concerns.

[23] Booth, Ken, *New Thinking about Strategy and International Security* (London: Harper Collins Academia, 1991), p. 43.

[24] Ibid., p. 44.

[25] Rummell, R.J., *Understanding conflict and war. Vols. 1-5*, in: Booth, Ken (1991), "Security and Emancipation", *Review of International Studies*, Vol. 17, No. 4, p. 323.

[26] Booth, Ken, "Security and Emancipation", *Review of International Studies*, Vol. 17, No. 4, p. 319.

[27] Bull, Hedley, *The Anarchical Society* (London: Macmillan, 1977), p. 22.

[28] Chilton, Paul, A., *The meaning of security*, in: Beer and Hariman, Op cit., p. 195.

[29] Dalby, Simon, *Creating the Second Cold War* (London: Pinter Publishers, 1990), p. 31.

[30] Dalby, 1990, Op cit., p. 16.

[31] Dalby, 1994, Op cit., p. 6.

[32] Walker, R.B.J., *History of Structure in IR*, in: Der Derian, James, 1995. Op cit., p. 319.

[33] Walker, R.B.J., (1990), "Security, Sovereignty and the Challenge of World Politics", *Alternatives*, xv, 3-27, p. 9.

[34] Ibid., p. 11.

[35] See Campbell, David, Op cit.

[36] Rosenau, James, "Probing puzzles persistently: a desirable but improbable future for IR theory", in: Smith, Booth and Zalewski, *International theory; positivism and beyond* (Cambridge: Cambridge University Press, 1996), p. 312.

Chapter 2
Reconstituting Sovereignty: The Creation of Dispersed Vertical and Horizontal Sovereignty

Having outlined human security as what *should* be the fundamental objective of International Relations, I now wish to critique, in theoretical terms, the means by which this goal may be achieved. Proceeding from the theoretical ethos introduced in chapter one, I maintain that International Relations must extend beyond the dual image of *us* and *them* in the interest of human security. The theoretical model constructed here creates scaffolding allowing us to imagine a bridge between the binaries of *us* and *them*. In a multi-ethnic state and/or in a state having undergone intra-state war, such as Bosnia, dichotomy intensifies human insecurity. The Westphalia model maintains that security can only be provided through order. The sovereign territorial state provides such a function by ordering its relations with itself and others, intra-state and inter-state relations, respectively. In ordering relations, states have come to define political identities in both spatial and monolithic terms. Therefore, the Westphalia model demands a spatially determined jurisdiction consisting of a monolithic cultural identity. The end of the Cold War, however, has resulted in the proliferation of identity and the permeability of space. In such an environment, nationalism, particularly intra-state nationalism has intensified, as evident in the Former Yugoslavia, Chechnya and Rwanda.

In responding to such intra-state war we are left with two policy options. Preponderant forces may attempt to re-create spatial closure and monolithic cultural identity, as Tudjman and Milosovic attempted in the Former Yugoslavia, and in so doing sacrifice the richness and safety of human existence for the sake of state survival. The second alternative, theoretically developed within this chapter, discounts order based upon spatial closure and preponderant monolithic identity, and rather develops new spatial and identity configurations. In a world of ethno-nationalism and fratricidal struggle, the nurturing of human security is clearly handicapped by the intensity of nationalism.

17

In countering nationalism, which prevents the bridging of binaries, a redefinition of space and a celebration of multiple identity membership is presented within this chapter. It is argued that if the structures of governance were to become more functional in nature, the state structure itself would invariably weaken. It is not enough, however, to implement some form of functional governance, although in theory it may provide a greater degree of human security, being both more responsive and closer to the needs of the people. The structural template of Mitrany's radical liberalism, can in itself however, do little to curtail nationalism, the fundamental cause of human insecurity in regions such as Bosnia. The reality remains that the structural failures of the Westphalian system will persist until social loyalties are "decoded" away from the state. Therefore in "decoding" loyalties away from the nation state structure, I forward a critical theoretical approach, which aims to disassociate territory from sovereignty. In this sense the fundamental building block of International Relations is challenged, that is the correlation between territory and sovereignty. It is argued that a functional approach to governance would aid such structural alteration in two principal ways. Firstly, functionalism would aid the process, by decoding loyalties from the state onto local horizontal platforms. Secondly, the very process itself of disassociating sovereignty from territory is based upon the premise that sovereignty may reside on different levels of the vertical axis allocated according to need. Hence, the structural changes associated with the functional approach simultaneously require and stimulate changes in systems of political loyalty.[1] The creation of this theoretical hybrid unites the private domain with the public. In other words it treats the demands of self-creation and human solidarity as equally valid.

Fusing the *Innenwelt* and *Umwelt*

The development of human solidarity, based upon a fusion between *Innenwelt* and *Umwelt*, is necessary in order to create human security. In unravelling this complex question, theorists such as Richard Rorty would say that we *create* solidarity. "In my utopia, human solidarity would be seen not as a fact to be recognised by clearing away "prejudice" or burrowing down to previously hidden depths but, rather, as a goal to be achieved. It is to be achieved not by inquiry but by imagination, the imaginative ability to see strange people as fellow sufferers. Solidarity is not discovered by reflection but created."[2] Human solidarity should not therefore be thought about in relation to innate human nature, ontologically or in a primordial sense. Human solidarity is to be constructed, as there is no *Spiritus Mundi*[3] that binds us all spiritually in a universal sense. Theorists have continually attempted to explain solidarity in terms of the *Innenwelt* or the *Umwelt*. For example Nietzsche concentrates on attaining self-fulfilment, through the use of the (*Ubermensch*) superman metaphor, concentrating specifically upon the individual (*Innenwelt*), whilst Marx develops a theory of fulfilment in a macro (*Umwelt*) sense. Again John Stuart Mill envisaged society as a collection of individuals, whilst Henri Saint Simon puts emphasis upon the organic nature of society.

I hope to reconcile the particularistic with the universal by synthesising the needs of the particular with universal requirements. It is only through such a synthesis that we can hope to challenge the human insecurities prevailing in society. In this regard we can only safeguard the particular (my personal security/emancipation) by firstly accepting universal responsibilities. We can only create true *human security* by responding to the needs of all society. This philosophical basis holds that true *human security* can only be achieved if we respond to universal obligation, in other words if we respond to duties beyond borders. Such a process involves a total reconstitution of our understanding of sovereignty.[4] Such a reconstitution is necessary as the current construction of sovereignty within modernity only serves to uphold the nation state[5] and thus serves as a dichotomising agent which forces us to concentrate upon "my nation" at the expense of the universal "human security". The bitter irony arises however when one realises that "my nation" can never be secure until such time as we create universal "human solidarity". A fusion between the particular and the universal is thus evidently required. The current structure of sovereignty prevents the fostering of human security, insofar as sovereign statehood both creates and preserves monolithic national identity. The conundrum arises however in attempting to develop a theoretical approach, which would both allow for a resolution of the underlying causes of nationalisms and consequently consolidate *human security*. While the idea of functional government found in Mitrany answers many of the problems posed by the failings of the Westphalia system, it is hampered by a territorial and monolithic system of political loyalties that still sustains a fundamentally state-based system. The development of a functional system of government would require an understanding and a modification of the form and system of loyalties that currently operates through the spatially defined, but monolithic, nationalism.

Creating Human Solidarity

The theoretical approach outlined herein aims to construct human solidarity between peoples. The theoretical approach promotes solidarity based upon duty and obligation, rather than basing solidarity upon feudal criteria, such as kinship bonds, hierarchical obligation, or upon modern criteria, such as the nation state, ethnicity or religion (in other words sentiment).

Instead the philosophical basis of the theoretical approach established within this chapter involves the acceptance of trans-national duties, founded upon the need for human security and directed in the knowledge that human solidarity is a necessity in order to prevent a proliferation of intra-state conflict. In this regard human solidarity should be seen as a responsibility rather than a sacrifice.[6] The inability of the international community to deal successfully with wars in Rwanda, Bosnia, Kosovo and Palestine points to the fact that the most feasible and indeed materially practical solution to the wars of the future, is in fact prevention.[7]

The human and indeed economic cost of conflict is so great that we must attempt to develop the mechanisms of war prevention. It is our *duty* to develop more responsive mechanisms so as to suppress the sparks of conflict. We must also lessen the chance of conflict, by constructing communities responsive to the needs of identities.

In executing such mammoth tasks, however, society must first come to realise that solidarity is a duty rather than a sentiment. It would appear that the essence of modernity has influenced the moral consciousness of world citizens to such an extent that increasingly many people seem to attest to the rationale that one cannot have duties to aid anyone but members of one's own society. In this sense, solidarity/responsibility tends to be conditioned by spatiality. "Responsibility is greatest to those at the center and trails off as one moves outward along a radius of the circles. According to such a view a number of compatriots take priority over other compatriots, but all compatriots take priority over non-compatriots."[8]

This dominant contemporary *epistime* sees nationality as the justifying grounds for the granting of priority. For example the "national" welfare state is seen as normal, while the majority would consider a "global" or "regional" welfare state as altruistic. Basing our responsibilities upon this form of moral consciousness fits closely to a Humean view, which assumes that the limits of one's "affections" or sentiments are the limits of one's obligation.[9] The fundamental difficulty arising from this approach presents itself when we ask the question, who is going to support non-compatriots. Who is going to support the world's refugees, most of whom are children?

Within this chapter an approach is theoretically developed capable of restricting the wild freedom of the external relations between nation states. The necessity of this analysis arises from the fact that nation states tend to conduct their external relations in a free manner in line with self-interest and sentiment. Such freedom has had a detrimental effect upon citizens of the world who have been victimised by such an approach. As the research in chapter four displays, there were many socio-economic criteria which pre-empted the conflict in the Balkans. However the international community held no duty, responsibility or right to the peoples of the Balkans, as self-interest and sentiment continued to mould the policy of nation states in the international community. It is therefore an imperative that a community of interests is created, based upon duty, in the international arena.

Creating Human Security, Based upon Duty

The cosmopolitan model,[10] which attempts to create human security, has obviously failed to become a realisation, mainly due to the preponderance of hegemonic nation states that have superimposed their own elitist interests and therefore have served to hamper the progress of a true cosmopolitan model. The ineffectiveness of the United Nations, caused mainly by its structural reliance on the nation state, manifests this fact. Because of the preponderance of hegemonic nation states within its structure,

> the UN, whose main mission is to foster peace and co-operation among states, has not succeeded in performing its essential mandated service: to be *a centre offering a political framework* necessary to deal with international conflicts and to harmonise the actions of states in other areas of international concern.[11]

In advocating human security, therefore, I am firstly promoting an approach in order to minimise the preponderance of monolithic identity enshrined by the nation state structure. The aim is to encourage the representation of multiple identities and community memberships alongside the dis-aggregation of authority away from state sovereignty. "Rather the definition and character of sovereignty becomes more diffuse and diverse and with it the status and conception of borders as the delimitation of sovereign authority and homogeneous community is opened to a consistent line of questioning."[12] In this way I am not only questioning realist dogmas, which promote a strong territorial state as a safeguard against malignant human nature, but also tackling the rationale of neo-realism, which accepts anarchy at the international level.[13]

According to neo-realist philosophy, "no spatial unit other than the territory of the state is involved in international relations. Processes involving sub-state units (e.g. localities, regions) or larger units (e.g. world regions, the globe) are necessarily excluded."[14] Instead, however, we should be attempting to create a system capable of encompassing multiple identities. Such an approach involves the deconstruction of sovereignty, as we know it. Sovereignty (as defined by modernity) is the tool utilised by the nation state so as to maintain its legitimacy over a particular space. The creation of legitimate/sovereign space gives rise to the inside/outside dichotomy. Security is to be found inside the state, whilst the outside represents danger and *real politik*. Security is then, by definition, the defense of a particular spatial sovereignty. The fundamental problem with this arrangement is that increasingly the nation state is unable to provide security and in fact the inside/outside dichotomy, created by our modern conception of sovereignty, has served to intensify human insecurity, as shown in chapter four. It is my ambition within this work to redefine the character of sovereignty, in a theoretical sense, so as to allow the fostering of *human security*.

In achieving such an objective, I forward the idea of constructing a dispersed horizontal and vertical form of sovereignty, which gives legitimacy to all peoples. Creating a dispersed horizontal and vertical form of sovereignty will enable the deconstruction of space, insofar as the legitimisation arising from the correlation between space and sovereignty would be eroded. Dispersed horizontal and vertical sovereignty channels an escape route that circumvents the territorial trap of modernity and consequently the binary between *us* and *them*.

Creating a Horizontal Dispersal of Sovereignty

It would seem that the prevalence of the nation state and national identity has prevented proper functionalist developments, which theorists like Jean Monnet had sought. In addition, the prevalence of the nation state has prevented the adoption of true *human security*, as nation states seem more concerned with maintaining their own distinct character, rather than providing true human security.[15] Horizontal sovereignty can lessen the significance of nation states, insofar as it "intrudes" upon the jurisdiction of the nation state in providing services and duties for peoples. Horizontal sovereignty can best be created through the use of a functionalist approach.

Functionalism has the ability to overcome the sovereign power of the nation state by constructing appropriate structures that are not territorially based, but instead based upon a *need*,[16] performed to improve the common welfare of society.[17] In developing the functionalist approach, David Mitrany puts emphasis upon the creation of many specialised, economic and social institutions.

Regarding war and conflict, Mitrany envisages war to be caused by particular circumstances. "But the solution to war is not simply a correction of such deficiencies: it is the process of dealing with such deficiencies within organisations which, it is believed, produced the new dynamic of peace."[18] Specialised organisation, therefore, must be introduced into a turbulent region, not only to rectify the immediate deficiency, but also to create a lasting peace by fulfilling long-term needs and duties. If the socio-economic inequities and discrepancies had been dealt with in the Balkans for example, it would have created a much more benign society, where dangerous ideologies would have found it difficult to gather support. In the words of Mitrany, "give people a moderate sufficiency of what they need and ought to have and they will keep the peace".[19]

As implied in the words of Mitrany, peace "is achieved through organisation around issues other than security as traditionally understood".[20] This can only be achieved successfully if we are to practically institutionalise a form of dispersed horizontal sovereignty, as needs and duties can often only be served by specialised actors that cross boundaries. Specialised non-state actors which concentrate upon providing a given need or duty, in essence deconstruct the sovereign authority of the nation state, insofar as they intrude upon its jurisdiction. Simultaneously such non-state specialised actors reconstruct sovereignty on a dispersed horizontal basis, insofar as specific actors now provide specific duties to all peoples in need of that given function. Such an approach would have the effect of de-legitimising the sovereign character of the nation state. Such an approach helps create a dispersed form of horizontal sovereignty, as specific non-governmental actors would have sovereign authority over specific duties on a trans-territorial basis. I intend to undertake a case study regarding the success of post-Dayton Bosnia in developing a form of dispersed horizontal sovereignty between peoples. In this regard, I wish to analyse particularly the degree to which the *Accord* institutionalises horizontal sovereignty, and secondly the degree to which functional institutions created outside the codification's of the *Accord* are helping to build civil society. It remains the case, however, that horizontal sovereignty, articulated by functional institutions, cannot succeed without the disassociation of territory from sovereignty. In order to be successfully established dispersed horizontal sovereignty requires an environment in which loyalties and identities are fluid and less monolithic. In short, people must be freed from the feeling that they need a specific territorial identity. A vertical dispersal of sovereignty can help create such human security through its ability to "soften identities". In essence a vertical dispersal of sovereignty holds the capacity to decode the national identity dynamic and therefore may bridge binary opposition, and ultimately create human security.

Creating a Vertical Dispersal of Sovereignty

The idea behind a vertical dispersal of sovereignty, through at least initially a territorially based form of devolution, is to take the first step towards redefining identity as a set of interlocking loyalties, rather than as solid blocks of colour. Loyalty to all may not be possible, but this does not mean that a spatially defined monolithic loyalty based around the state is, therefore, the only alternative. Rather the answer lies in non-hierarchical and overlapping system of loyalties, some spatial and some not, that are simultaneously specific, but also do not create sharp distinctions between *us* and *them*. A cobweb of loyalties, analogous to Hobhouse's cobweb of functions, would allow for loyalty to be particular, but by making each political loyalty just one of a number of loyalties there is no sense of exclusion. A vertically dispersed sovereignty begins this process by creating a situation in which, at least politically, individuals define themselves differently depending on circumstances and situations.

Within the case study undertaken in chapter six, I analyse the ability of the *Dayton Peace Accord* to institutionalise a dispersed vertical form of sovereignty, which potentially could lessens the degree to which the nation state, as the ubiquitous sovereign authority, constructs a single homogenous identity. A vertical dispersal of sovereignty would allow all identities to articulate and represent themselves within a dispersed structure. Such a dispersal of sovereignty is clearly required in order to limit the preponderance of an elite who claim, under the current system, to represent the whole. Such representation is of course a clear fallacy, because even

> if all states had exactly the same rights, and even if they were somehow provided with equal possibilities of development, this would still be a world in which power and decisions about international regimes are heavily concentrated in the hands of a few.[21]

In order to create a system capable of representing all peoples, a form of global humanism must be promoted. Of course such a utopian ideal cannot simply be created, or more accurately central state sovereignty cannot simply be wished away. I have therefore put forward a theoretical approach (dispersed vertical sovereignty), which may eventually realise this goal in practice. Vertical sovereignty structurally allows the articulation of the sovereign voice of all peoples, all identities, at local, regional, federal and supranational level.

Thomas Pogge has forwarded this idea of a worldwide multilevel scheme of political units, which requires a vertical dispersal of sovereignty.[22] Dispersing political authority over territorial units would decrease the intensity of the struggle for power and wealth within and among states. According to Pogge the institutional development of a vertical form of sovereignty would force today's developed countries to take on responsibility regarding duties. Initially such a proposal must appear utopian, the idea of distributive justice comprising of a world community, within which distribution takes place. However, what Pogge proposes is far more complex than "Robin Hood economics", and differs considerably from merely taking wealth from the rich and giving to the poor. Pogge's institutional approach would not be so much concerned with the equitable redistribution of a given pool of resources, "but rather how to choose or design the economic ground rules, which regulate property, co-operation, and exchange and thereby condition production and distribution".[23] Pogge proposes that this could be best achieved through the institutional development of a vertical dispersal of sovereignty that is both responsive to needs and accountable to duties. Such a dispersed vertical form of sovereignty would certainly weaken monolithic identity and the strength of the territorial state, and in this way help create more inclusive communities capable of accommodating all voices.

> Thus, persons should be citizens of, and govern themselves through, a number of political units of various sizes, without any one political unit being dominant and thus occupying the traditional role of state. And their

political allegiance and loyalty should be widely dispersed over these units: neighbourhood, town, county, province, state, region, and world at large.[24]

The formation of dispersed vertical sovereign structures would certainly create a more responsive and thereby democratic environment. The current system which holds the nation state as its unit of analysis perpetuates interstate and intrastate rivalries, insofar as it arbitrarily demarcates inside from outside and only allows the sovereign nation state a voice, thus alienating so many more citizens within its territory. The creation of space, through the formation of dispersed vertical sovereignty would help reduce oppression, insofar as the institutional framework would give all identities a voice with which to speak. One of the significant advantages of a dispersed vertical form of sovereignty is that, unlike a world state, it does not attempt to suppress/homogenise the nation, culture, identity, rather it protects the interests of communities at all levels of the vertical equation. In this sense it liberates local identities and consequently reduces the propensity to engage in ethno-nationalism. Considering the intensity of the ethnic war that took place in Bosnia (1991-95) it is necessary that the peace agreement (*The Dayton Peace Accord*) can create human security, so as to provide the space necessary to allow a multi-ethnic society to live in peace and dignity. The fostering of human security is, however, dependent upon successful governance, based upon adequate representation and responsiveness to need. In achieving this objective dispersed vertical institutions capable of representing identities and social needs, together with horizontal structures capable of supporting identities and needs would form the basis of good governance.

Representing Multiple Identities

With the deconstruction of the sovereign nation state and the reconstruction of vertical and horizontal sovereignty, a theoretical route is being channeled capable of circumventing the nation state and threatening communitarian politics, which traditionally has served as a dichotomising agent and thus an instigator of insecurity. This process involves firstly questioning the "givens" enshrined within modernity, such as, why might it be right that the territory of the world be divided by arbitrary lines on a map? This urges one to question ontological truths, such as the validity of territory and autonomy derived from the Peace of Westphalia and formalised in the doctrine of nation state sovereignty. It is through this doctrine of nation state sovereignty that the idea of spatial exclusion arises, which defines "us" and "them" through membership of the sovereign territorial state. The rise of the postmodern condition and its penetration into International Relations theory asks us to "problemise" such borders, viewing them not as givens but as obstacles to emancipation. Territorial borders serve only then to intensify insecurity, by enclosing what they perceive as homogeneous communities. We need to accept the growing importance of multiple identities and multiple community membership to the normative agenda of International Relations, as recognition of multiple identities is both recognition of what is, and provides us with the challenge to reconfigure sovereignty according to identities. I believe multiple identity membership can be created if we install a degree of horizontal and vertical sovereignty. Synthesising as a unit, dispersed vertical and horizontal sovereignty holds the ability to represent all peoples at all levels, thus creating human security.

These two approaches compliment each other and allow for the development of *human security*, based upon a functional ethos. Human security differs considerably from the more traditional definition of security, which in Hobbesian mode, was envisaged as an absolute value. "In exchange for providing it the state can rightfully ask anything from a citizen save that he sacrifice his own life, for preservation of life is the essence of security."[25] The Hobbesian ethos of security therefore allows for suppression of liberties in the interest of order. A homogenisation of society, through the formation of a sovereign nation state is the ideal, even if this involves (as in the case of Turkey, Israel, federal Yugoslavia) the alienation of identities. Human security as an analytical tool puts much less emphasis upon the suppression of identity and rather emphasises the liberation of identities. With this emphasis upon the emancipation and representation of identities, human security is in many respects postmodern in character. "The postmodern state is one in which society plays a dominant role in politics, and the state, heavily constrained by law and openness, is more its ringholder and servant than its master."[26] With the implementation of dispersed vertical and horizontal sovereignty, nation state sovereignty would effectively be forced to relinquish its power position. Instead the myriad of identities within society would articulate sovereignty. In effect such a dispersal of sovereignty would relinquish the ability of the state to *include* and *exclude* peoples by subverting sovereignty from the state. In essence the creation of dispersed vertical and horizontal sovereignty represents new alterations in power configurations, replacing the power configurations created under the Westphalian model, and thus enabling us as a society to challenge the conflicts of the present and the future.

Conclusion

Functional organisations cannot create a new system of loyalty on their own as long as nationalism remains the dominant form of political loyalty. Rather, a process of mixed territorial loyalties needs to be established first, which will negate against functional organisations becoming merely another forum for inter-state competition. The horizontal functionalism of Mitrany has the potential to sustain a system of interlocking identities, but only once the strong pull of exclusive national identities has been decoded (at least partially) by vertical dispersal of sovereignty. The creation of institutionally decentralised governance possesses the ability to create human security, insofar as the institutional structures both emancipate the individual, by fulfilling needs, and safeguards the whole through the creation of vertical structures. The creation of such structures will have the effect of institutionalising duty and obligation and thereby establishing a more pro-active and responsive society. The proliferation and growing professionalism of NGOs certainly marks a step in this direction.[27] In order to tangibly mark the prevalence and usefulness of this critical theoretical approach within the field of IR, the next logical and indeed necessary step involves constitutionally codifying and recognising the function of non-state and sub-state actors.

The augmentation of non-state/sub-state actors have catalysed the process of decentralisation, democratisation and empowerment at local level, insofar as non-state/sub-state actors have the ability to reach the poorest areas, promote local participation, operate at low costs and contain an ability to be adaptive and flexible and thus in essence create human security. In fact "most NGOs place a high premium on the formation of new groups, or the strengthening of existing groups, a means of raising awareness, empowering the poor and promoting the goal of self-reliance".[28] The penetration of non-state/sub-state actors into the state and their promotion of *human security* could erode the preponderance of monolithic identities and unitary spatiality, by empower other identities in other spaces.

Notes

[1] Ashworth, L. and Keane, R. (2000), "Creating Wastelands Called Peace: The Failure of State Security and the Functionalist Alternative", International Political Science Association, XVIII World Congress, Quebec.

[2] Rorty, Richard, *Contingency, Irony, and Solidarity* (Cambridge: Cambridge University Press), 1989, p. xvi.

[3] The spirit or soul of the universe, with which all individual souls are connected through the "Great Memory", which Yeats held to be a universal subconscious in which the human race preserves its past memories. See Yeats, W.B., *The Second Coming*.

[4] Early expressions of our understanding of sovereignty can be found in the writings of Jean Bodin. Writing in 1586, Bodin defined the state as "a lawful government of several households, and their uncommon possessions, with sovereign power". Sabine, "A history of political theory", in: Couloumbis, A., Theodore and Wolfe, H. James, *Introduction to International Relations Power and Justice* (New Jersey: Prentice-Hall, Inc, 1982), p. 54. E.H. Carr makes the point in *The Twenty Years' Crisis* that the term sovereignty which was invented after the break-up of the medieval system so as to describe the independent character of the authority claimed and exercised by states, was likely to become more blurred and indistinct in the future. See Carr, E. H., *The Twenty Years' Crisis* (New York: Harper and Row Publishers, 1964), p. 230.

[5] The nation state is upheld by the ubiquitous jurisdiction of internal and external sovereignty. "Internal sovereignty concerns the supreme and lawful authority of the state over its citizens. External sovereignty, on the other hand, refers to the recognition by all states of the independence, territorial integrity, and inviolability of each state as represented by its government." Couloumbis, A., *et al*, Op cit., p. 55.

[6] Der Derian, James, *International theory: Critical investigations* (Basingstake: Macmillan Press, 1995), p. 353.

[7] Increasingly the United Nations is putting greater emphasis upon conflict prevention by way of preventative diplomacy and preventative deployment. Also non-governmental organisations such as International Alert, Partners for Democratic Change, and Saferworld engage in conflict prevention.

[8] Shue, Henry, *Basic Rights: Subsistence, Affluence and US Foreign Policy* (Princeton: Princeton University Press, 1980), pp. 134-135.

[9] See Hume, David, *A Treatise of Human Nature* (London: Fontana Press, 1972), pp. 318-322.

[10] Danilo Zolo in his work *Cosmopolis* manifests the limitations of all cosmopolitan models from the Holy Alliance, to the League of Nations and the United Nations. In his view they represent "a hierarchical institutional model which superimposes the hegemonic tactics and aspirations of a narrow elite of superpowers on the sovereignty of all other countries". See Zolo, Danilo, *Cosmopolis* (Cambridge: Polity Press, 1997), p. 164.

[11] Roberts, Adam and Kingsbury, Benedict (eds.), *United Nations, Divided World* (Cambridge: Clarendon Press, 1988), p. 136.

[12] Williams, John (1998), "The Ethics of Borders and the Borders of Ethics: International Society and rights and duties of special beneficence", Paper presented to the Department of International Relations, University of St. Andrews and the ECPR Standing Group on IR/ISA Third Pan-European Conference on International Relations, p. 4.

[13] See Waltz, K.E., *Theory of International Politics* (New York: Random House, 1979).

[14] Agnew, John and Corbridge, Stuart, *Mastering Space* (London: Routledge, 1995), p. 82.

[15] See Keane, Rory (2000), "A new vision for Europe: A challenge to the nation state", Institute on Western Europe, 17th Annual Graduate Student Conference, Columbia University.

[16] "Need" in this context is founded upon David Mitrany's observation of the common basis of need across the world.

[17] Nobel Peace Prize winning NGO, *Medicins sans Frontiers*, is a good example of a functionalist institution that intrudes upon the jurisdiction of nation states so as to improve the common welfare of society.

[18] Groom, A.J.R. and Taylor, P., *Frameworks for International co-operation* (London: Pinter Publishers, 1990), p. 129.

[19] Ibid., p. 130.

[20] Ashworth, L. and Long, D.   (eds.), *New Perspectives on International Functionalism* (London: Macmillan Press, 1999), p. 113.

[21] Hoffmann, Stanley, *Duties Beyond Borders* (New York: Syracuse University Press, 1981), p. 145.

[22] Pogge, Thomas (1992), "Cosmopolitanism and Sovereignty", *Ethics*, 103, October.

[23] Ibid., p. 56.

[24] Ibid., p. 58.

[25] Lynn-Jones, Sean, M. and Miller, Steven, E. (eds.), *Global Dangers-Changing Dimensions of International Security* (Cambridge, Mass.: M.I.T. Press, 1995), p. 16.

[26] Ibid., p. 187.

[27] In 1992, NGOs provided $8.3 billion in aid to developing countries, representing 13 percent of development assistance worldwide.

[28] Marcussen, Henrik, Secher (1996), "NGO's, the State and Civil Society", *Review of African Political Economy*, No. 69, p. 412.

Chapter 3
The Nation State: A Constructed Entity

Part I: The Changing Face of Sovereignty

Only by calling into question the ontological status of the nation state within International Relations theory can its deconstruction be properly legitimised. To this end the "naturalness" of the nation state is held open to question within this chapter. The theoretical road mapped out casts doubt on acceptance of the nation state as the base unit of analysis within International Relations. Countering modernist nationalist ideology, which proclaims a long unbroken narrative of the nation's past, the genealogical approach undertaken deconstructs such a single interpretation of events, which has given supreme authority to nationalism and the nation state structure. In fact using the tool of genealogy enables the deconstruction of the grand narrative of history. The history of nationalism and the nation state is shown rather to be only one reading of events, which has gained legitimacy over space and time. The nation state has thus been *constructed* in a *spatio-temporal* sense as an axiomatic truth. It is the aim of this chapter to manifest the constructed nature of the nation state as a truth. Such a process is required so as to legitimise the replacement of the traditional nation state with a more emancipating structure. Traditional International Relations theory has attempted in its short life to develop theory around the truth of the nation state. The fundamental flaw in this approach arises from the inability to see the nation state as an *intertext*.[1] Rather, the nation state has been accepted as the subject matter and subject actor within International Relations. In coming to comprehend its dimensions the discourses and texts that prop up its ontology must be critically investigated.[2] For example, theorists have failed traditionally to deconstruct the meaning and essence of "truths", such as state, sovereignty, identity and nationalism, which the nation state very much depends upon for survival. In recent times this failing has promoted certain theorists to utilise a genealogical approach in their will to knowledge.

Obviously not satisfied with the mode of reality constructed within modernity, which tends to "heroize" the present,[3] and thus implicitly shapes and edits all histories to conform to a present simulated reality, daring theorists have attempted to break the mode in the will to counter truths. As vividly articulated by Foucault: "It is no longer a question of judging the past in the name of a truth that only we can possess in the present, but of risking the destruction of the subject who seeks knowledge in the endless deployment of the will to knowledge."[4]

Nietzsche's work on Morals and Bartelson's work on Sovereignty are prime examples of this approach. They firstly deconstruct given truths, and secondly present accounts of the incidents which shaped and influenced the development of truths throughout time. A genealogical approach, therefore, differs considerably from archaeology, which does not dare to question preconceived truths, and in fact often imposes a monotonous finality to history. A genealogical approach, on the other hand, gives a pride of place to historicity and, in typical poststructuralist fashion, attempts to destabilise, and therefore renders open to question, all claims to an absolute foundation. Theorists such as Richard K. Ashley have used this approach to challenge History as *Le Texte General,* and thereby contend that each aspect of history must be comprehended as an *intertext.* In this regard no piece of history can be fixed, finally bound and homogeneous in its meaning.

This process of deconstructing the nation state is indeed an arduous task, given that such terms as the state, sovereignty and national identity are interwoven and assumed as ontological facts. For example, the concept of sovereignty rests upon the principle of the state, which is enshrined within modernity. Added to that the whole ethos of modernity prevents any critical analysis which might take place, as modernity enshrines the creation of a reality which appears real and true, but which on analysis is no more than a mere simulation[5] and/or imagination.[6] Modernity represents a simulation of truth and knowledge that hampers any real analysis. Onuf articulates this point vividly, showing that the acceptance of modernity as truth has hindered analysis of concepts enshrined within modernity, such as sovereignty. "With modernity taken for granted, the conceptual intelligibility and normative implications of sovereignty went largely unchallenged."[7] Deconstructing such a concept as the sovereign nation state is thus far from a straightforward task insofar as the essence of such a concept is built upon simulated reality and indeed perceived innate ontological facts.

The Background to this Genealogical Approach

A genealogical study attempts to understand how the past is formed and shaped by present concerns. Rather than attempting the impossible, the quest for a suprahistorical perspective above and outside history, a genealogical study is both more realistic and indeed more innovative in attempting to order a history of how the present state of affairs was formed.

Friedrich Nietzsche executes this approach formidably in his acclaimed work *On the Genealogy of Morals*. Here Nietzsche gives a new direction to the discipline of morals. For example in the first essay "Good and Evil, Good and Bad" Nietzsche accounts a genealogy of morals through an analysis of the feudalistic hierarchy where the noble masters proclaimed themselves "the good" and where the aristocracy formulated value judgement, often to their own advantage. "We noble ones, we good, beautiful, happy ones!"[8] Meanwhile the nobles viewed the common man simply as unhappy in direct contrast with themselves. What is significant about this study arises from the fact that Nietzsche took an ontological given, morals, and showed how they have been constructed over time and indeed space, in this case by the nobility. The concept of morals therefore cannot be considered as an innate suprahistorical given. He goes on to account how the Jews were the first to challenge the aristocratic value equation of morals which maintained that "*good = noble = powerful = beautiful = happy = beloved of God*".[9] The Jews, according to Nietzsche associated morals instead with the poor, wretched, impotent or sick. Of course Nietzsche rejects the Christian-like account of morals developed by the Jews, and instead viewed this form of morality as the essence of resentment. "...This *need* to direct one's view outward instead of back to oneself – is of the essence of *resentment*: in order to exist, slave morality always first needs a hostile external world".[10] However, what is of most significance here is the fact that the Jewish definition of moral runs counter to that of the aristocrats, thereby opening up the ontological status of morality itself. The two varying accounts of morals vividly augment the fact that there is never a pure historical origin, and hence no unbroken continuities or succession in history.[11]

A Genealogy of Sovereignty

As a starting point, I intend to draw on the genealogical works of Jen Bartelson in relation to sovereignty. I intend to analyse whether sovereignty is intrinsically related to the formation and perpetuation of the state. I hypothesise, in fact, that sovereignty is much more than a protective shell for the state and instead sovereignty actually creates the state, demarcating the world within the state from the world of states.

Bartelson's work on sovereignty is of particular interest, as both the concept of sovereignty and the state are closely interrelated. Sovereignty was described by Hinsley as the "final and absolute political authority in the political community".[12] It appears thus at a very basic level that sovereignty is governed to a large extent by authority. How is this authority composed? Who holds such authority and how has the composition of such authority transformed over time? These were the questions Bartelson confronted in executing a genealogical approach. As Nietzsche once noted, only that which has no history can be defined. Bartelson elaborated on this, making the point that history is a mode of writing rather than a mode of being. In this regard Nietzsche and Bartelson point to the fact that history has been constructed. The past has been regulated, edited and indeed mutilated so as to explain either the here and now or perhaps the future. Sovereignty as a principal arm of state legitimacy has traditionally been excluded from interpretation and analysis, and in fact has acted totally as a sponge concept. For example realist IR theorists make reference to sovereignty, so as to legitimise and explain territoriality, international law and exclusion, without ever deconstructing the term itself.[13] With Bartelson's deconstruction of sovereignty we begin both to question its ontological status and begin to understand its relationship with the state and indeed state formation. Through a genealogical analysis we may also come to realise that the natural state is in fact a constructed entity that has taken on its character over time and space. Rather than progressing from a hermeneutic perspective, attempting to interpret the past as it actually was, I hope through the use of genealogy to account and analyse those historical accidents and collisions that have both constructed and have put the modern state beyond the reach of analysis.

The Changing Face of Sovereignty

As a starting point I wish to develop upon sovereignty from an anticendentic perspective. I analyse specifically the direct and indirect precursors that have shaped the development of sovereignty. It was not really until the late medieval era, and particularly the Renaissance, that we see the development of popular sovereignty as a concept.[14] Onuf sees the emergence of sovereignty at this point as being due to the fact that the medieval world as an overarching social construction had ended, the anachronistic structure of the Medieval Age having been replaced by a multitude of thriving republics and principalities. Nevertheless although this is the case, it is of interest to note that even in the late Renaissance period sovereignty (or authority) still resided with the King or ruler. It is even more significant to note that the concept of the state, as we know it today, did not exist in this period. This arises from the fact that there was less an emphasis upon a spatially demarcated territory and more an emphasis upon the vertical relationship between God, the King and the subjects'. It was thus the King, as God's ambassador, that held sovereignty. "The Great Chain of Being" thus still existed and sovereignty rested at the apex creating an unquestioned cosmology.[15] The King, as God's ambassador on earth, was thus invariably enshrined with a sense of moral legitimacy. This we can see implicitly displayed in the popular culture at the time. Indoctrinated in much of Shakespeare's work, we get a sense of the legitimate and noble King, who must constantly fight for supremacy over the illegitimate and tyrannical serpent, so as to save the Kingdom from upheaval and disunity. For example, the illegitimate Macbeth, who subverted the chain of degree, is unable to sustain his hold on the Crown and in time Malcolm the rightful and legitimate heir to the throne dethrones Macbeth through force, thus restoring justice and the great moral order.

It is evident from the above that sovereignty had little to do with the litany of concepts we associate it with today, such as nationalism, patriotism, culture, ethnicity and so on. Instead sovereignty resided in and through the King, as he represented the medium of transmission between God and subject. This doctrine descended directly from God through the Gospel. "Thou art Peter and upon this rock I will build my church."[16] The King in this sense represented two bodies (the King's two bodies[17]) one of earthly and one of divine character.[18] What is of most significance in marking the Renaissance from the Classical Age was the evolution in the theory of sovereignty. In the late Middle Ages and in the Renaissance, as previously stated, sovereignty was a mark of superiority or a sign of divine origin. In the Classical age, however, the concept became associated with a new mode of knowledge. This new mode of knowledge was based to a large extent upon science, which in the 17th century was becoming ever more influential.[19] Such atemporal scientific approaches began to emerge in the writings on statecraft by theorists such as Bodin and Hobbes. We can thus detect the emergence of a new discursive practice, a system based upon the forming and validation of empirical statements about states. At this stage we begin to detect the emergence of the rationality that prevails over our present day perceptions and articulation of the state. The growth in rationality in time destroyed the traditional notion of sovereignty, replacing it instead with sovereignty based upon territorial delineation, expressed by the nation state and nationalism.

From the Sovereign King to the Sovereign People

The genealogical approach clearly facilitates a questioning of sovereignty. It becomes evident that nations and peoples were not always used to define sovereignty. We see from the analysis undertaken that the modern conception of sovereignty did not exist under feudal rule, as subjects had divided loyalties. In fact the development of the nation is the fundamental criterion, which realised the conceptualisation of sovereignty, as understood within modernity. Sovereignty today, legitimises itself by calling upon the nation/people as its guarantor. The fruits of the genealogical approach thus make clear that the advent of nation is based upon the erosion of the sovereign great chain of being. The nation is, therefore, neither primordial nor fixed, but rather the result of power alterations and social transitions.

 The doctrine of the divine right of Kings, where sovereignty rested in one body, continued relatively undisturbed up until the seventeenth century. Slowly and particularly after the Treaty of Westphalia the privilege of divine Right was restricted to certain states and from this period the state began to strengthen in character, at the expense of the feudalistic hierarchy. The decline in the feudalistic system also affected the essence of sovereignty and from this period sovereignty entered a process of metamorphosis, as the divine sovereign authority began to be replaced by "the Enigma of Representation". This enigma of representation saw the formation of a representative parliament that eventually replaced the divine right of Kings. However, it would firstly be necessary to "invent" a sovereign people. This was only possible if a new ideology, a new rationale, a new set of fictions was created to justify a government in which the authority of Kings stood below that of the people or more specifically, their representatives. This process was indeed slow and arduous, but can be most vividly displayed in England, for example, from the year 1660 to 1690. During this time period we slowly begin to see the divesting of sovereignty from the King and simultaneous cloaking of sovereignty on the Parliament. The Exclusion Crisis of 1679-80 marks a reversal in this process.[20] This crisis revolved around the fact that most Tories continued to see the King as having divine rights and therefore supremacy over the Parliament. The Whigs on the other hand, merely saw the King as "part" of the system.[21] This crisis culminated in the glorious revolution of 1688, which affirmed the Whiggish view of Monarchy, as merely part of the system. The transferring of sovereignty from King to representatives was at this stage well under way.

One must pose the question as to why the duty towards God (represented formally by the Pope and later by the King) gave way to the rights of man? In answering this question it is first necessary that we do not over-exaggerate the alteration in power that occurred. For example, we should be aware that even the old ideology of divine right had not generally excluded "the people" from a nominal role.[22] Secondly, ironically the enigma of representation had little to do with "power to the people" but instead power to the peoples' representatives. These public representatives, for example in the House of Commons in Britain, were exclusively from the upper middle class and comprised of untitled landholders, merchants and rich professionals. Therefore, the transferring of sovereignty from the King to the people was thus merely an enigma, as sovereignty merely transferred from the King to the elite representatives. These parliamentary representatives, such as Henry Parker, legitimised and rationalised their authority, by making reference to "the people" they represented. The transferring of sovereignty from King to citizen during the 17th century was thus at a very symbolic level and represented no real alteration in the feudalistic hierarchy of power.

The Decentralised World of the Middle Ages

In the Middle Ages the feudal system based on kinship and common law ruled. Such a system, based upon micro-communities and porous borders, paid little reverence to spatial demarcation. That is not to say that people were wholly nomadic, particularly in Western Europe kinship groups were sedentary and displayed a strong link with the land. However, it was also the case that all sections of European populations did roam in the Middle Ages, including entertainers, cattle herders, (for example, Welsh farmers took their cattle in droves to London) royal law courts and Roma.

The process of spatial delineation was somewhat slower in the Orient and even by the Middle Ages it was visible that no real spatial consciousness had developed. However neither could it be said that these peoples wandered aimlessly, but instead followed the trail of resources. "The primitive nomad who depends for survival on what he can find…must know the territory in which he roams: locales of water holes, where certain plants grow, the habits of game, etc."[23] In time these nomads stationed themselves in one given place where they could find adequate resources. Lattimore's study of the Mongols showed that this establishment of fixed private ownership led to the parcelling and repartitioning of tribal territory. This same process occurred also in Western Europe, but at an earlier stage. Spatial demarcation was of course an ongoing process and as testimony to that we see the constant drafting and redrafting of boarders in every epoch. For example, the Treaty of the Pyrenees decided where the exact boundary line between Spain and France would be drawn in 1659. What is most significant regarding the demarcation of specific territories is that it created one sovereign to which all citizens of the territory were answerable.

Under feudal rule, on the other hand, this concept of sovereignty did not exist, as subjects had divided loyalties to both church and state. In Germany before the Thirty Years War, according to C. V. Wedgwood a population of about twenty one million depended for its government on more than two thousand separate authorities.[24] Similarly, the Duke of Lorraine, which was nominally within the Empire, also owed allegiance to the King of France. However with the gradual formation of delineated states, sovereignty began to be personified and directed towards one entity. As exclusive sovereignty increasingly resided with King or Ruler, there was need for the development of a central authority to deal exclusively with internal and defense administration. Here we see the initial embryonic development of the modern nation state.

Forging State Centralism – A Growing Consciousness of Spatial Delineation

It is important to understand that knowledge, a socially and historically constructed practice, creates the state. There cannot be an omnipresent truth regarding the state, therefore, as its condition and construction varies over space and time. It is thus not possible to ascertain a basic understanding of the state without taking into account the role of knowledge. Foucault would maintain that it is important to account the mutual interdependent nature of power and knowledge. It appears thus that power both presupposes and produces knowledge.[25] Alterations in power configurations, therefore, result in new ways of thinking and new forms of social organisation. This interrelationship between power and knowledge was significant in the construction and orientation of sovereignty in the Renaissance, the Classical age and in Modernity, according to Bartelson.

Bartelson's discussion of these three periods is of interest firstly insofar as they are all seen as possible midwifes to the birth of the modern state. The Italian city documented by Machiavelli with its diplomats and war strategies is often cited as the embryonic origin of the modern state. Again the Classical age which saw the Thirty Years War, and subsequent signing of the treaties of Westphalia, is often associated with the birth of the modern state system. Whilst thirdly, there are those that maintain the modern system did not come to be until the modern nation state was formulated, aided by the birth of nationalism during the French revolution. This hypothesis is often referred to as the modernity hypothesis.[26] The insightful work carried out by Bartelson in relation to how sovereignty transgressed in character over these periods not only manifests the interrelationship between power and knowledge, but also gives us a deeper understanding as to how the state, as we know it today, came into existence.

Although the King maintained divine character, the Renaissance is often cited as the period that saw the formation of the state. This however is not fully true, as the sovereign state was not individuated as an object in itself at this stage. Significantly, however, the Renaissance did mark the birth of the inside/outside dichotomy (to borrow R.B.J. Walkers terminology). The inside/outside dichotomy certainly represents a general theory of the state, and imposes a demarcation or delineation of territories. The inside/outside dichotomy created, however, differs quite considerably in character from Walker's meaning, which relates to an identity versus difference conflict. The inside/outside dichotomy of the Renaissance according to Meincke, "does not presuppose an outside other than a heterogeneous and largely unknown outside of a *Respublica Christiana*".[27] The "outside" therefore does not represent foreign, as it would today, but instead simply represents the unknown. During the late Renaissance, thanks predominantly to Machiavelli, we see the development of the modern delineated state as an object of human knowledge and as an instrument of power and *virtù*. According to Machiavelli the good man, who wants to preserve his city or maintain its political order, must be a good architect and a good orator.

> Such good, wise and powerful men, 'good and prudent,' 'good and merciful,' who populate so many pages of the *Istorie, the Discorsi* and the

Arte della guerra, exhibit the features of the republican civil man, the good
man who reforms the institutions and laws of the city to the greatest benefit
of all citizens.[28]

Machiavelli as accounted here, to a large extent helped define the role and
reason of the state and in this regard promoted the replacement of the
religious divine hierarchy with a scientific art of the state. Machiavelli
maintained, thereafter, that natural law could be superseded by a more
coherent, rational and scientific state. The direct effect of Machiavelli's
massive influence on the art of the state is that it eroded the old state system
which put little influence upon the world outside the state, and substituted a
state system which was very much conscious of its borders and its
neighbours.

The Westphalia system, as a response to the conflict and disorder
resulting from the Thirty Years War, was yet another significant turning
point in the development of the modern territorial state. The Westphalia
system codified and legally demarcated specific states. By the Classical
Age therefore we see the development of a "system", as articulated both by
Grotius and Pufendorf, of a fundamental moral or legal unity underlying
the accentuated division into particular states.[29] Having analysed state
formation and its relationship with sovereignty on a wholly theoretical
level, it has become evident that the interrelationship between power and
knowledge was significant in the construction of sovereignty. Sovereignty
(authority) in the Middle Ages and for most of the Renaissance period
resided with the all-powerful King. This arose from the fact that there was
less an emphasis upon a spatially demarcated territory and more an
emphasis upon the vertical relationship between God, the King and the
subjects. It was only really in the late Renaissance that the modern
delineated state as an object of human knowledge and an instrument of
power developed, thanks predominantly to Machiavelli. Finally, in the
Classical Age sovereignty became associated with a new mode of scientific
knowledge, which rationalized the process of state formation.

The Centralist Policy of Emerging Absolute Rule

One can trace the emergence of the modern national mindset to the late
Renaissance and early modern period. It was initially this period that gave
rise to collectivist policy, often based upon kinship bonds, common
language (or dialect), and the centralist regime of emerging absolute rule.

The centralist policy of emerging absolute rulers was of particular importance. Such preponderant policies often involved the severing of certain kinship bonds, or the suppression of certain languages or dialects. In this way unnatural absolute rule paved the way for a homogenous society, based upon a common language and a codified hierarchy. The absolutist unification policies also meant the liquidation of dissenters and the general acceptance of one common creed. From this period onward, we therefore witness the forming of common identities. These common identities helped fuse the state and society together and thus helped cultivate the ground in which the modern nation state grew. The development and forming of common identities varied considerably from state to state and was dependent upon many variables including the strength and command of the absolute sovereign authority, the size of the state, the number of ethnic groups in a given territory and the relationship between the central state and regional feudalistic Lords. The formations of centralist monarchies did, however, to a greater or lesser degree, occur in all European states, and thereby laid the foundation for the eventual development of nationalism.

As previously stated, in the Middle Ages the dominant form of political organisation in Western Europe was the Germanic Kingdom, based more so upon loyalties rather than abstract concepts or impersonal institutions. Significantly these Middle Age Kingdoms were less restricted to time and space than the modern state. For example, some Kingdoms lacked continuity whilst others moved about fantastically in space; in a few generations the kingdom of the West Goths jumped from the region of the Baltic to that of the Black Sea to that of the Bay of Biscay.[30] The embryonic development of the modern centralised state can, however, be found in the midst of this period and can be roughly traced back to the period 1100 to 1600. It is in this period that we see the crystallisation of centralisation policy.

In this section I examine the ways in which the power of the state increased in early modern Western Europe, and how this in turn shaped political opposition to the state. "The process of state-building helped create the political context within which nationalism could develop and the national sentiments which nationalists could subsequently exploit. It was not, however, itself justified in nationalist terms."[31] The process of empire building cultivated the expression of discontent amongst those peoples who felt alienated from the given superstructure. The expression of such discontent had not as of yet taken on a nationalist sentiment. Rather people were more concerned with political, economic or religious alienation that resulted from the preponderance of empire.

Alterations in the concept of sovereignty resulted in new power configurations and brought about the discourse of nationalism, which will be analysed more specifically in the next section. Nationalism has never really been fundamentally questioned by dominant paradigms within International Relations theory because of its considered natural and omnipresent truth. As outlined above, Bartelson succeeded in deconstructing the naturalness of the nation state by manifesting the historically determined and "man" constructed character of sovereignty, which the nation state requires in order to legitimise itself. Working on this premise, I set about deconstructing the naturalness of Balkan nationalism in the sections that follow. Therefore, a genealogical study is undertaken in order to uproot the grand narrative of Balkan nationalism. In this regard it is shown that the constitution and reconstitution of sovereign power in the Balkans created an environment where nationalism fostered.

Part II: The Case of Serbia, Croatia and Bosnia

The Fostering of Nationalism

According to Montaigne, the renowned Renaissance humanist, "unless some one thing is found of which we are *completely* certain, we can be certain about nothing".[32] As outlined above, there is nothing *completely* certain or ontological regarding the character of sovereignty. The *balkanisation*[33] of peoples into nation states is both the result of alterations in the meaning and understanding of sovereignty, as expounded by Bartelson. Having asserted that there is nothing natural or ontological regarding the modern territorial sovereignty, it follows that the unquestioned reality of nationalism must also be scrutinised, as nationalism is based upon a perceived right to sovereignty. Of course nationalism as very mush a modernity construct sees sovereignty in territorial terms. International Relations theory has been perhaps premature in accepting the principle of nationalism as axiomatic. Particularly, Wilsonian ideals of *national self-determination* put beyond analysis the real question, namely whether nationalism is authentic in and of itself. Rather than simply accepting nationalism as axiomatic, I intend instead, by means of a genealogical approach, to analyse whether the will to nationalism based upon territorial delineation, is in fact real? In this sense the axiom of nationalism is challenged and is shown rather to be a product resulting from alterations in the character of sovereignty. According to Baudrillard, "seduction is that which extracts meaning from discourse and detracts it from its truth".[34] The discourse of nationalism, which legitimises the territorial state, must be brought into question. We must attempt to move beyond discourse, as all discourse conspire and seduce to combat meaning. In this vein a genealogical analysis is utilised, as a means of stripping the discourse of nationalism. It is generally accepted that the former Yugoslavia provides an example of a region ravaged by fervent nationalism from the period of the Ottoman and Habsburg empires. The reality of ethnic hatred and long standing animosities between Serbs and Croats may easily allow us get ravelled up in the myth of nationalism. By utilising a genealogical analysis I hope to counter nationalism and prove that the balkanisation of the South Slavs was catalysed by the constitution and reconstitution of sovereign power in the region. Through the use of a genealogy a counter-history is established, capable of destroying the *power-knowledge*[35] nexus, which legitimises nationalism and thereby accepts the nation state as ontological and *completely* certain. In pursuing this genealogical analysis of Balkan nationalism I concentrate broadly upon how power factors altered the character of sovereignty, which in turn crystallised nationalism. The reason for paying particular attention to power factors derives from the results of the genealogical analysis conducted into nation state formation in section one of this chapter. Within that study the genealogical approach uprooted the influence and changing face of power (defined as sovereignty) as the fundamental force responsible for nation state formation.

The Sovereign Serbian Kingdom

Affiliation into various religious denominations, from Bogomilism[36] to Orthodox and Roman Christianity catalysed the process of distinctiveness between various Slavic groups. The Serbs were first referred to as a distinct group in the Balkans in the writings of the Byzantine emperor Constantine VII.[37] The development of Serbian political unity was a slow and arduous journey, as society was fragmented into micro clans or tribes, each under its own *zupan* (chieftain). A process of consolidation based upon strategic marriages and domination eventually allowed Stephan Nemanja to become Grand *Zupan* of Raska in 1169. His reign marks the birth of a Serbian sovereign principality free from Byzantium infiltration. Medieval Serbia reached its zenith in the fourteenth century during the reign of Dusan (1331-55). Dusan helped solidify the Kingdom, which was achieved to a large extent by giving the Serbian Church an enhanced status. However Dusan's ambition led eventually to the capitulation of the Serbian Kingdom. He had his eyes set upon the Byzantine throne and the fragile Byzantines were eventually forced to call upon the help of the Ottoman Turks to assist them in holding the Serbs at bay. The Byzantine throne had become quite weak after the Byzantine army was defeated in 1071 by the Turkish power in the decisive battle of Manzikert.[38]

Dusan withstood the eastern invaders in 1345 and 1349 but within thirty years of his death most of his Kingdom had fallen to the Ottoman's. Stefan Uros IV "the Weak" (1355-1371) and Jovan Uros (1370-1373) were the last two Nemanjics' to serve as autonomous Kings of Serbia before Serbia was brought under the Turkish yoke and became a vassal of the Sultan following the battle of Kosovo Polje in 1389.[39] The development of a cohesive Serbian Kingdom in the Middle Ages, concurs with Bartelson's genealogical account of sovereignty, as outlined in section one of this chapter. According to Bartelson it was really only in the late Medieval Ages and Renaissance period that we see the development of sovereignty as a concept. However, it is explained that the emergence of sovereignty in no way marks the birth of modern nationalism or the nation state, as the Great Chain of Being still existed. We see this reality in the case of Serbia where the relationship between the people was still based upon a vertical demarcation between God, King (in the Serbian case Dusan) and man. In this regard a consciousness of a spatial demarcation had not as of yet developed.

The Sovereign Croatian Kingdom

"In 924 Tomislav, *zupan* of Nin, declared himself King of the Croats and established a kingdom free from both Frankish and Byzantine rule."[40] The development of the Kingdom of Croatia followed a similar pattern to that of Serbia. Under the reign of Zvonimir (1077-1095) the choice of Roman Christianity was taken on board. The Croat kingdom attempted to remain independent from the influence of both the Byzantines and the Holy Roman Empire. Croatian sovereignty was however from the very beginning in a fragile state. This fact was compounded by the close and frequently hostile relationship between Croatia and Hungary. Following the death of the ruling Croatian Prince Zvonimir, Prince Kalman of Hungary gained the Croatian throne. Soon after in 1106 Kalman acceded to the Hungarian throne thus effectively bringing Croatian under the jurisdiction of Hungary.

Here lies the advent of conflict between Magyars and Croats that would in time assert itself as a bitter struggle for power and dominance over where exactly sovereign power should reside. The complexity of the Croatian question became even more complex when Turkey managed to annex much of Croatia in 1493. The Croatian nobility fought bravely and saw victory against the Turks in the fields of Krbava, only to be defeated in a great massacre not unlike that suffered by the Serbs a century earlier at Kosovo. Subsequently what remained of Croatia was taken over by the Habsburg Empire, following the defeat of the Hungarians at the hands of the Ottoman's.[41]

The Kingdom of Bosnia and Herzegovina

Between the ninth and eleventh century much of Bosnia and Herzegovina was incorporated in the kingdoms of both Serbia and Croatia and even Macedonia. "The first distinctly Bosnian state emerged in the late twelfth century under the legendary Ban Kulin (1180-1204)."[42] His fascination and adherence to the Bogomil heresy caused Hungary to interfere on behalf of the papacy. In fact adherence to Bogomilism should be considered as an influential factor in the development of a specific Bosnian sovereign identity. As articulated in section one, the *Inside/Outside* dichotomy enshrined by the nation state did not exist in the Medieval period. Rather the Medieval principality did not presuppose an outside other than a heterogeneous and largely unknown outside of a *Respublica Christiana*. All peoples therefore who affiliated to the Christian club were seen as a part of "us". It is in accordance with this philosophy that Joan of Arc proclaimed that, "all those who fight against the holy kingdom of France fight against the Lord Jesus".[43] The acceptance of the Bogomil heresy in Bosnia, served in this regard as an instrument in shaping and defining Bosnian sovereign identity, as "outside" the Christian club. For over a century, the Bans or chieftains in Bosnia were forced to accept Hungarian penetration, as they attempted to suppress the Bogomil heresy. Finally, suppression of the Bogomil heresy was achieved to a large extent under the administration of Ban Stjepan Kotromanic, who assumed office around 1318. He had a close relationship with the Hungarians and was therefore rewarded with assistance against various Croatian nobles. He even managed to annex Hum from the Serbs in 1326. The Ban did not interestingly interfere with the Orthodox institutions there. What is most significant regarding the reign of Kotromanic was his support of Catholicism by way of the Franciscan missions. "There had been no Catholics, at least no Catholic clergy or organisation, in the center of his state for nearly a century. By 1342 the Franciscan Vicariate of Bosnia was established; eventually its territory was to include all those parts of southeastern Europe where Franciscans worked."[44] Kotromanic died in 1353 and was succeeded by his teenage nephew Tvrtko 1 (1353-91) who brought Bosnia to its zenith in the medieval period. He was crowned King of Serbia and Bosnia in 1377 and by 1390 Tvrtko had added Croatia and Dalmatia to his royal title. Interestingly all the battles that took place between Kings and nobles in Bosnia were fought over territory. Not once did medieval Bosnians fight one another on religious or ethnic grounds. Eventually after the battle of Mohacs in 1526 virtually all of Bosnia and Herzegovina fell to the Ottoman sultan. Many Serbs and Croats thereafter who had lived in Bosnia fled to Habsburg controlled territory, whilst the majority of those who stayed behind, especially the adherents of the Bogomil faith, accepted Islam.

The Wandering Character of Sovereign Identity

Let us pause a moment to consider the identity labels that may be applied to communities in Bosnia. Interestingly we do not find Bosnians referring to themselves as Bosnian Serb, Croats or Muslims, as is the case today. "If they wanted a major label, they called themselves Bosnians. We cannot say that they perceived this term as an ethnic one. More likely, it signified the geographical region they came from.... Often these people in Bosnia also used regional identity labels like Hum, Donji Kraj, etc."[45] Two of the principal reasons as to why they were not spatially and ethnically conscious arise firstly, because they put greater emphasis upon the vertical hierarchy, as explained earlier. Secondly, peoples tended to channel their sovereign identity towards the universal church, either Byzantium or Rome. It must be strongly emphasised that none of these early states were *national* in character.

> The government represented primarily alliances of strong nobles around a central leader... Feudal loyalties rested on the mutual interest of the most powerful men in the state in the protection and extension of its frontiers. When his personal fortunes were better served by opposition to his rule and alliance with an enemy power, a noble could easily shift his allegiance.[46]

The modern notion of the nation state had not developed at this time. This fact is manifested in the reality that states tended to be spatially mobile. For example, Croatia had its first centre on the Dalmatian coast and by the sixteenth century Zagreb (Agram) had become its major city. Again there were no ethnically pure people in any specific region, particularly prior to the Ottoman and Habsburg invasions.

> In each region the population represented a fusion of original inhabitants with subsequent invaders, an amalgamation achieved through military conquest by a stronger group, the absorption of one people by another owing to the weight of numbers, or the acceptance of another language because of the cultural attraction offered by a more advanced civilisation.[47]

It was still very difficult at this point to envisage what national form the various Slav groups would develop. Would there develop a single Slav nation, just as Angles, Saxons and Jutes were becoming one at the same time in England?[48] All that could be certain was that three specific Kingdoms with military strength and a core territorial area had been created. Thus we know of a Croat kingdom from the time of Tomislav of Knin in the tenth century, a Serb kingdom flourishing in the thirteenth and fourteenth centuries, and a Bosnian kingdom in the fourteenth and fifteenth centuries.

The Influence of Foreign Rule in Constituting a Modern Conception of Sovereignty

After a period of foreign rule a clear and consistent theme regarding the development of distinctive Slavic cultures and identities became evident. The role of foreign imperial powers had a catalysing effect leading to a widening of the cultural difference between Slavic peoples. For example, the Kingdom of Byzantium influenced the adoption of Orthodox Christianity in Serbia. The Byzantine missionaries Cyril and Methodius played a large part in bringing Christianity to the Slavs and are often referred to as the "Apostles of the Slavs".[49] Again the Ottoman's played a colossal role in directing the development of Serbia. Had the Nemanjics continued to reign supreme without the infiltration of the Turks, the Serb's Slavic tradition would no doubt have taken on an altogether different formation, in the sense that its sovereign sense of self would have been constructed in a less imposed manner, rather than configured merely as an opposition to the external "other", namely the Ottoman empire

In relation to Croatia and Bosnia and Herzegovina, the same applies. The evolution of Croatian consciousness was consistently shaped by Hungarian sovereignty over the region. Again, Croatia's proximity to the Holy Roman Empire influenced the brand of Christianity, which it finally adopted. Ottoman and Hungarian annexation of the lands of Bosnia and Herzegovina conditioned its development. In a general sense the semi-feudal system developing in the lands of the South Slavs was thwarted and directed by the infiltration and ambitions of external forces. The degree to which national distinctiveness can be considered innate or primordial must therefore seriously be called into question. The character of indigenous evolution was conditioned to a large extent by the continual influence of foreign rule. Two overriding social features of the Turkish system of government imprinted those mass areas under Turkish control. They were the *millet* system and the *devsirme*. Each religious community or *millet* was placed under the supervision of its own leader, who acted as an agent for the Turkish government, regarding the collecting of taxes etc. The *devsirme* was a much less enlightenment aspect of Ottoman custom and involved the compulsory enrolment of Christian boys into the military. They were not only forced into service but also were compelled to become Muslims and to learn Turkish and the Koran. In addition to the forced conversion of Christian boys through the *devsirme* system, there were also voluntary conversions that took place gradually. The austere *devsirme* system caused many Slavs to convert to Islam and helps explain the presence in modern Bosnia of a large Slav-speaking Muslim community. The Ottoman administration utilised the *millet* system as a means to collect revenue. This was achieved principally through a poll tax known as *cizye*. The bulk of this tax was paid by the Christian *raya* (flock). The effect the Ottomans had upon the economy is of particular interest. Firstly, the Turkish conquest had the effect of withering away the traces of non-agricultural enterprises that had previously existed in the Ottoman controlled areas of the Balkans. Instead the Ottomans developed the feudal system with the development of large privately owned estates known as *ciftliks*. The Muslims owned and controlled the *ciftliks*, while the Christians farmed them. As the demands from the Ottoman Empire increased, the Muslim owners of the *ciftliks* consequently put greater pressure upon the Christian *raya*. Such extortion would obviously in time lead to revolt.

Causes of Feudal Disintegration

"From the decline of the Roman Empire until at least the end of the Middle Ages, ties of lordship, kinship, community, and religion were the primary basis of social organisation in Western Europe."[50] People used to see themselves as part of a larger order. In some cases, this was a cosmic order, a "Great Chain of Being", in which humans figured in their proper place along with angels, heavenly bodies, and our fellow earthly creatures. Cracks began to appear in the great hierarchical Chain of Being in the late Middle Ages and even more so with the birth of the Enlightenment. The yearning for a more rational, and thereby profitable, administration resulted in the disintegration of the feudal hierarchy. As discussed earlier, the emergence of this form of rationality had considerably developed by the seventeenth century, when theorists such as Newton began to develop theories of natural science, based upon a sense of reason and rationality. Traditionally imperial powers supported their lords in the struggles they might encounter against the peasants' etc. Increasingly however the central power saw it necessary to restructure their relationship with Lordships so as to renovate society and/or to increase state revenue.[51] The degree to which the central imperial powers infiltrated and strictly codified relationships with feudal Lords, in comparison with earlier periods where the feudal lords were allowed a greater degree of autonomy, derived from the increasing preponderance and consequently ubiquitous sovereign power practiced by imperial empires. Another major cause of the decline of the feudal system was the escalating and indeed omnipresent dissatisfaction among Serfs, slaves and peasants. Struggles fought for centuries over the stigma of servitude to higher authority eventually intensified resulting in revolution. The intensification of discontent had to a large degree come about due to the increase in commercialisation. Two points are of significance here; firstly commercialisation altered the character of lordship. Lordship came to be based less on political power and status and more so upon economic relations. Feudal lords were therefore increasingly more interested in material gain. Secondly, commercialisation in making some peasants wealthier, not only enabled them to buy there way out of obligations, but also raised their aspirations and expectations.[52] The upper indigenous classes therefore began to aspire towards sovereign power, which eventually would result in the disintegration of feudalism. Here we see how socio-economic inequality and power relations culminated, resulting in upheaval in who should and would hold overriding sovereignty.

Feudal Disintegration and the Rise of Nationalism: A Case Study of Serbia, Croatia and Bosnia

The medieval period ends with the Yugoslav lands been divided up between Turks and Habsburgs. The existence of practiced and intact cultures, fostered in the Medieval period by the Croatian, Bosnian and Serbian principalities played a catalysing role in the articulation of national consciousness that developed under the occupation of the great sovereign imperial powers, namely Ottoman and Habsburg. One may rightfully pose the question as to why the articulation of nationalist consciousness developed in this period and not in earlier times when the Croats, Serbs and Bosnians were also influenced by external imperial forces, namely the Byzantium empire, the Holy Roman Empire and particularly the Hungarian preponderance over Croatia? The answer to this question lies in the fact that the Ottoman and Habsburg empires were the first to rationalise their regimes of operation in the interest of greater control, authority, infiltration and thereby material gain. Such an approach was necessary so as to sustain the imperial empires in the face of external threats, growing and more technologically advanced armies and modernisation. "The Ottoman situation was comparatively more dangerous, since foreign states did contemplate the dismemberment of the empire."[53] The outcome of the process of rationalisation interestingly resulted in the break down of the feudal chain, the Great Chain of Being that had regulated life so effectively in the Middle Ages. The modern and ubiquitous procedures that developed in its place brought imperial penetration into the local level. Through an analysis of the modernisation processes developed by the Ottoman and Habsburg powers, we begin to see how and why a nationalist consciousness might be created as a defensive mechanism against the destruction of the old order.

The Serbian Experience

In Serbia itself the Nemanjich monarchy (1166-1373) played an important function in laying the foundations of an identity that could later be expropriated to the cause of nationalists. The church also made the transition from medieval antecedents to modern nationalism. The Serbian national church, through the use of the local language and through the power and function of the Patriarch helped solidify Serbian identity. The

Sultan further augmented the process with the restoration of the patriarchate of Pec in 1557.

As outlined through example in section one, the centralist policy of absolute rulers was of particular importance in sowing the seeds of nationalism. Such preponderant policies often involved the severing of certain kinship bonds, or the suppression of certain languages, religions or cultures. As a reaction to such preponderance common identities were forged. These common identities helped fuse society together and thus helped cultivate the ground on which the modern sovereign nation state grew. The growing Ottoman commercialisation of landholding in Serbia was beginning to have a negative effect, particularly upon the upper Serbian classes. In addition, peasants increasingly wished to till their own land and profit from their toil.

Also, from the seventeenth century onward, military service became professional. The professional infantry, the *janissaries*,[54] were under no obligation to the local population and increasingly began to show less obligation to the Sultan. (As their relationship with the Sultan was increasingly based upon economic ties rather than kinship ties.) The vast size of the Ottoman Empire and its structural and administrative ineptitude allowed the rebellious *janissaries* to ravage the peasant Serbs. The Porte was challenged therefore more so by its own motley array of ayans, beys, Christians and Muslim military leaders than by the Serbs. Finally by 1804, with the failure of Selim III to contain and control the *janissaries*, the frightened peasantry rose up against them.

In 1801 Selim III had been beheaded by the *janissaries*. This act of aggression arose principally because Selim in his first decade of reign had attempted to appease the Serbs by granting them a degree of self-government. Selim's enlightened policy stems perhaps from his correspondence with Louis XVI of France concerning his plans for reorganising the army. Meanwhile the enlightening process occurring in Western Europe, particularly the ideal of romantic nationalism influenced the middle classes in Serbia. "Romantic nationalism based on the demand for recognition of cultural identity was a sentiment which moved the educated middle classes."[55] The Serbian peasants, who accounted for the bulk of the population, had more pressing matters, particularly relating to material oppression. Added to that, the *janissaries* were increasingly plundering and abusing the local Christian peasantry. The enlightened policies initiated by Selim, including the *oberknezovi* (local parliament) being given more power, increased rights for the Orthodox churches. However, such enlightened policy together with the permission to form a local Serbian militia actually only served to intensify the taste of self-government and indeed the self-confidence of the Serbs.

Finally, in 1804, the Serbs were catalysed into action by the "slaughter of the *knezes*" (leaders) in January and February of 1804 when a number of prominent Serbs were murdered. "Under Karageorge's leadership, the frightened peasantry of Shumadiya rose against them [the *janissarie*]. By the time they had rid the province of the *janissaries* they had also, however, carried out a real revolution which destroyed the foundations of Turkish power in Serbia."[56] The 1804 revolution was *not* an uprising based upon naked nationalism. Instead, it was a reactive revolution against the naked aggression of a hostile force, namely the *janissaries*. The great and heroic victory, the leadership of Karageorge, plus the already galvanised identity of the people aided the development of a nationalist consciousness thereafter.[57] The Ottomans eventually managed to claw back to power and dominance in Serbia, however in 1815 a second Serbian rising occurred under Milos Obrenovic. This time the Serbs were successful and by 1830 had earned independence.

Inspired by the spirit of the Enlightenment ethos that had captivated Western Europe, Serbia also witnessed a cultural reawakening. "In 1814, inspired by Herder's *Stimmen der Volker*, Vuk (Karadžić) produced a volume of Serbian national songs, in the preface to which he drew attention to the need for a standardisation of language."[58] Indeed the articulation of romantic nationalism was a process that was occurring all over Europe. In England for example as outlined earlier, the protestant leaders of early modern England developed a distinctive view of English history, and buttressed their position by the invocation and manipulation of memory.[59]

The Croatian Experience

As in the case of Serbia, feudalism in Croatia was a native development that emerged out of tribal and communal structures. Although native in origin, Croatian feudalism was surrogated and put to the use of the Hungarian feudal structure in 1102 after the proclamation of the union of the two crowns. Again the Turks surrogated the structure in 1493 when they attacked the heart of Croatia. Finally the Croatian feudal structure was taken over by the Habsburg Empire after the defeat of the Hungarians at the hands of the Turks at the battle of Mohacs in 1526. The attempt to liberate the South Slavs from the Turks had made the Croats more aware and sensitive of their past. This awareness of the past was indirectly nurtured by the more enlightened (although still despotic) policies introduced by the Habsburg monarch Joseph II (1765-90), who extended the benefits of education to the Croatian peasants. Sensitivity towards culture and language developed by way of education, and the revolutionary ideals of Enlightenment implanted by Napoleon's Illyrian ideal laid the basis for the development of a national consciousness. The penetration of Enlightenment ideals and the development of the educational system in Croatia resulted in a change of attitude among peasants. "There was less inclination to believe that God had assigned each individual a role in life and that people should fulfil their functions without complaint."[60] The economic hardship experienced by the peasants in the 1840's, particularly due to bad harvests resulted in uprising and revolt. The success of the peasants was quite limited, however, as they had no real organisation or indeed a clear aspiration. The real engine room of the 1848 revolution was the middle classes and the indigenous nobility. They claimed to speak for the "nation" and the "people", but the reforms desired by the majority of the peasants were of low priority.

The Bosnian Experience

The breakdown of feudalism in Bosnia marked the birth of ethnic consciousness in the region, which again resulted in the fostering of nationalism. The Sultan in his attempt to modernise the army and his administration faced severe opposition from the *janissaries* in Bosnia. The Sultan finally abolished the order after much threat and consideration. The powerful *janissaries* unsurprisingly refused to accept the edict and vicious conflict ensued. Finally the sultan managed to eliminate the corps as an organisation in Bosnia in 1827. "Of course, each intervention (especially if it employed violence) left a legacy of alienation and hostility among the local Muslims, making it less likely that they would accept a new reform or even supply the troops demanded of them."[61] Therefore, there were many conflicts between the local Muslim elite and the Sultan.

From 1850 onward, however, rebellions took on a mass character. "Until 1850 disorders had usually pitted the local Muslim elite against the central state authority; in the years after 1850, unrest took the form of peasant uprisings (chiefly Christian) against local landlords and local officials."[62] Interesting such revolts, as in the cases of Serbia and Croatia, were not based upon fervent nationalism, or indeed even patriotism, but instead upon economic issues. The reason for such intense solidarity was issues such as the demands for more regular payments of taxes from the peasants and the internal conditions of the peninsula. The situation from the eighteenth century onwards was so chaotic that both Christians and Muslims were forced to organise their own defences. The 1875 uprising led eventually to Great Power intervention, which placed Bosnia under equally austere Austrian control. It is no doubt true that the peasant revolts in Bosnia gave the peoples of Bosnia a sense of common identity. External forces, namely the Franciscans and the Orthodox millet, however, slowly fragmented such common identity. The Franciscans, who were mainly of Croatian origin, promoted nationalist sentiment and ideology that had already appeared in Croatia. They promoted closer association with Croatia and aspired to Bosnia one day joining Croatia. Meanwhile, the Orthodox community, influenced by the newly autonomous Serbian principality, began to see themselves as Serbian. The Muslims as a community were in constant decline and were increasingly stigmatised by the Christians who saw them as the remnants of foreign oppression. At this stage we see that spatial consciousness had come of age and increasingly ethnicities began to organise themselves in terms of territory and borders. Increasingly the development of nationalism, brought about by social upheaval, resulted in the augmentation of mass political parties.

Growing Awareness of Ethno-Consciousness

By the late-nineteenth century, the development of a consciousness based upon ethnicity was firmly in place. In the years between 1850 and 1878 the revolts were based upon social conditions.

> Even though the landlords were Muslims and most of the peasants Christians, this should not be seen as a case of religious war. Since the causes that drove them to revolt were the conditions of serfdom under which they suffered, it makes sense to see the main underlying causes as being social or class based.[63]

The real instigator of nationalism then in Bosnia finds its roots in socio-economic factors. Of interest, however, is the fact that, by the nineteenth century, Bosnia, which up until that period denoted a geographical region whose inhabitants came to share many similar values and characteristics, suddenly became divided along ethnic lines. The development of such ethnic consciousness was obviously developed by nationalists. Its accuracy however was less than tantamount considering that the population was greatly mixed as a result of various migration and indeed wholesale religious conversions over the epochs. Secondly, as already clarified in the earlier sub-section, the Bosnians as a Slavic group only came over time to affiliate into the three religions in question by way of imperial conquest and force. To speak therefore in the nineteenth century of Orthodox Bosnians, Catholic Bosnians or Bosnian Muslims, for example, as an ethnic group was both unnatural and historically inaccurate. Why were the soils of Bosnia so fertile as to allow the seeds of nationalism to take root in such a steadfast manner in the nineteenth century? In delving into the substance of such a question one principal factor must be kept in mind, namely the years of turmoil (1875-78). Historians tell us that these years mark a watershed in Bosnian history, comparable to 1776 in America, 1789 in France and 1917 in Russia. Historical *fact* nevertheless contradicts such a narrative of reality, as the austere Ottoman regime was simply replaced by the austere Austrian regime.[64] Rather, the years following the peasant revolt were very significant, however, as they mark a watershed in thinking. The social protests directed at the Ottomans mutated into desire based upon an ethnoreligious mindset. It appeared that Serbian and Croatian nationalisms were beginning to take root in Bosnia. "The success of the Serbs in 1867 and the Greeks in 1866-69 had shown that the Balkan people could, with profit, take matters into their own hands."[65] The Austro-Hungarians attempted to quell this development under the leadership of Finance Minister Benjamin von Kallay, by promoting the notion of Bosnianism. However, ethno-consciousness had already reached an advanced stage, and in October 1907, encouraged by a liberalised Austrian stance towards political expression, the Serbian National Organisation was formed, asserting a political program that Bosnia and Herzegovina was Serbian land. Interestingly, a year later a number of Croatian Catholic intellectuals met and created the Croatian National Union. Their party program claimed that Bosnia and Herzegovina was Croatian land, declared that the Muslims were Croats and called for a unification of all Croats. Then in 1906 the Bosnian Muslim landowners created a formal political party, the Muslim National Organisation.

Conclusion: Balkan Nationalism

By the end of the nineteenth century, Balkan nationalism had matured. Whilst initially unrest was based upon material problems, the struggle of uprising and revolution caused the original goals to mutate. Changes in several domains of social life, which were irreducible to one another, including material relations caused the original goals to mutate. The domain of social episteme, created by the feudalistic and thereafter-imperialist powers, constructed the mental equipment by means of which people reimagined their collective existence. There are myriad factors, which catalysed this change. These include the fact that the great romantic nationalist doctrines of Western Europe had influence upon Balkan peoples in the late nineteenth century. The theories of German philosophers such as Johann Gottfried Herder were devoured with relish. Herder believed that art, music and literature etc. were manifestations of a people (*Volksgeist*).

Fundamentally, social forces culminated, in the cases of Bosnia, Croatia and Serbia, resulting in the constellation of nationalism. In the case of the Habsburg Empire, the yearning for a more rational and thereby profitable administration resulted in the disintegration of the feudal hierarchy. The *anomie* resulting from the erosion of the old order created a great degree of discontent amongst the colonised peoples, which came to be expressed by way of nationalist aspiration. These new regimes tended to be even more centralist in nature and thereby alienated the peoples to a greater degree. In the case of the Ottoman Empire, the Sultan attempted to rationalise the regime in the interest of greater control and justice. The nobility and the *janissaries* had plundered and abused the peasants of Serbia both economically and socially, which resulted in mass peasant revolt in 1804. This revolution in itself was not based upon naked nationalism, but was a reactive revolution against the naked aggression of a hostile force. It was particularly the middle classes in Serbia who gave the movement a national character. They had benefited from Selim III enlightened policies; they were also more organised and possibly were more influenced by the romantic nationalism of Western Europe. In the case of Bosnia, socio-economic factors were to the fore in forwarding the birth of nationalism. Pre-1850 the feudal order of Bosnia was in a state of disarray with many conflicts between local Muslims, the *janissaries* and the forces of the Sultan. After approximately 1850 the uprisings took on a mass character. The cause of such intense solidarity was catalysed by such issues as the demands for more regular payments of taxes and such material matters plus the unruly behaviour of the *janissaries*. By the late nineteenth century, nationalism in the Balkans had synthesised and structured itself by way of nationalist political parties. At this stage of mature development it would be very difficult to erode nationalist aspirations within the Balkans. The best that could be achieved in the post-war period was to dampen the spirit of nationalism by redirecting the *Volksgeist* towards pan-Slavism.

This was attempted through the development of a royal dictatorship, namely the Kingdom of the Serbs, Croats and Slovenes and later by a communist dictatorship, under the charismatic Tito. However, the sense of nationalism had already taken root and lay fertile underneath a thin surface. In confronting nationalism, a more complex theoretical formula than pan-slavism or *brotherhood and unity* would have to be uncovered. In uncovering such a formula, the process of genealogy opens up new avenues of exploration. Through the process of genealogy, the character of sovereignty is shown to be responsible for the construction nation and nationalism. In this sense a reconstitution of sovereignty may provide a means by which to deconstruct nationalism.

Notes

[1] An intertext is a relation between two or more TEXTS which has an effect upon the way in which the intertext (that is, the text within which other texts reside or echo their presence) is READ. Nationalism as an intertext is in relation with such texts as identity, culture, linguistics and economics etc. and therefore is difficult to deconstruct. See for definition Hawthorn, Jeremy, *A concise glossary of contemporary literary theory* (3rd edition London: Arnold, 1998), p. 116.

[2] "Poststructural practices have been used critically to investigate how the subject – in the dual senses of the subject-matter and the subject-actor – of international relations is constituted in and through the discourses and texts of world politics". Der Derian, James and Shapiro, J., Michael, *International/Intertextual Relations* (Lexington: Lexington Books, 1989), p. ix.

[3] See Baudelaire's account of modernity, in: Foucault, Michel (ed. Paul Rabinaw), *The Foucault Reader* (New York: Pantheon Books, 1984), p. 40.

[4] Ibid., p. 97.

[5] The simulation of reality is a concept dealt with primarily by Jean Baudrillard. See Baudrillard Jean (ed. Mark Poster) *Selected Writings* (Cambridge: Polity Press, 1988).

[6] Benedict Anderson notes the use of imagery in fabricating the formation of nations and the spread of nationalism. In this sense human agency and imagination play a pivotal role in creating the nation. See Anderson, Benedict, *Imagined Communities: reflections on the origin and spread of nationalism* (London: Verso, 1983); See also Ringrose, Marjorie and Lerner J. Adam, *Reimagining the Nation* (Buckingham: Open University Press, 1993).

[7] Onuf, N. G. (1991), "Sovereignty: Outline of a Conceptual History", *Alternatives* 16, p. 425.

[8] Cohen, Mitchell and Fermon, Nicole (eds.), *Princeton Readings in Political Thought* (Princeton, New Jersey: Princeton University Press, 1996), pp. 467-468.

[9] Nietzsche, F., *On the Genealogy of Morals* (Translated by W. Kaufmann, New York: Vintage Books, 1967), p. 34.

[10] Cohen, Mitchell and Fermon, Nicole (eds.), Op cit., p. 467.

[11] Bartelson, Jens, *A Genealogy of Sovereignty* (Cambridge: Cambridge University Press, 1995), p. 75.

[12] Hinsley, F.H., *Sovereignty* (New York: Basic Books, 1996), p. 26.

[13] In chapter 19 of Morgenthau's *Politics among Nations*, the role and function of sovereignty in International Relations is outlined, however Morgenthau fails to question the character or constructed character of sovereignty. See Morgenthau, Hans, *Politics among Nations* (New York: McGraw-Hill, 1985) [1958].

[14] Aspirations to popular sovereignty can be found in Aristotle's belief in the "collective wisdom of the multitude", and in Marsilius's writings on a secular law govern state. See McCelland, J.S., *A History of Western Political Thought* (London: Routledge, 1996), pp. 142-147.

[15] See Ashworth, Lucian M., *The Roots of Westphalia* (Limerick: University of Limerick Press, 1997).

[16] Matthew, XVI, 18-19.

[17] Kantorowicz, Ernst. H., *The King's two Bodies: A study in medieval political theology* (Princeton: Princeton University Press, 1957).

[18] For example, Shakespeare shows King Hamlet in an earthly form as he died from poisoning, and in a supernatural light when he returns as a ghost.

[19] See chapter one for an account of the birth of rationality and its permeation into the political sphere.

[20] It was during this conflict that the names Tory and Whig were heard for the first time and thus marks the beginning of the modern party system.

[21] Ball, Terence, *Transforming Political Discourse* (Oxford: Basil Blackwell Press, 1988), p. 34.

[22] The People here refer only to the educated elite and Nobles.

[23] Murty, T.S. "Frontiers, a Changing Concept", in: Kratochwil, F. (1986), "Systems, Boundaries and Territoriality", *A Quarterly Journal of International Relations*, Vol.XXXIX, No. 1, Oct, p. 16.

[24] Wedgwood, C.V., *The Thirty Years War*, in: Kratochwil, F. (1986), "Systems, Boundaries and Territoriality", *A Quarterly Journal of International Relations*, Vol.XXXIX, No. 1, Oct, p. 16.

[25] Foucault, *The Foucault Reader*, 1984.

[26] See Bartelson, Op cit. for a more detailed account.

[27] See for a more comprehensive account Scott, D., *Modern History* (Boulder and London: Westview, 1984).

[28] Viroli, Maurizio, *From Politics to Reason of State* (Cambridge: Cambridge University Press, 1992), p. 173.

[29] See Wight, Martin, *The System of States* (Leicester: Leicester University Press, 1977).

[30] Strayer, R. Joseph, *On the Medieval Origins of the Modern State* (Princeton: Princeton University Press, 1970).

[31] Breuilly, John, *Nationalism and the State* (Manchester: Manchester University Press, 1993), p. 76.

[32] Toulmin, Stephen, *Cosmopolis* (Chicago: The University of Chicago Press, 1990), p. 42.

[33] So marked has been the historical turbulence in the Balkans, that the term "to Balkanise" has come to mean fractionisation into small inimical units, See Jelavich, Charles and Barbara, *The Balkans in Transition* (Berkeley: University of California Press, 1963), p. 1.

[34] Baudrillard, Jean, *Selected Writings* (Cambridge: Polity Press, 1988), p. 149.

[35] According to Foucault "forms of power-knowledge…are means to exercise power and at the same time rules which establish knowledge", nationalism by this definition can be taken as such a form. So as to destroy the preponderance of nationalism a counter-history

(genealogy) is required to unmask constructed memory, see Visker, Rudi, *Michel Foucault Genealogy as Critique* (London: Verso, 1995).

[36] Bogomilism was a dualist and docetist sect that arose and flourished in medieval Bulgaria, the Bogomils derived their name from their founder, the priest Bogomil (Theophilus). In 1180, Stephen Nemanja of Serbia began to check Bogomil activity in his kingdom. Bosnia and Herzogovina became the strongholds of Bogomilism during the XIII century; it was often associated with nationalism.

[37] His influential work *De administrando imperio*, refers specifically to the Serbs.

[38] Poultan, Hugh and Taji-Farouki Suha (eds.), *Muslim Identity and the Balkan State* (London: Hurst and Company, 1997), p. 223.

[39] The Serbian principality of Zeta (present-day Montenegro) experienced a somewhat different path towards development. Although the people of Zeta were culturally indistinguishable from the Serbs, they escaped infiltration by the Ottoman yoke and thereby experienced a distinctive and very different path than Serbia, which had become a vassal of the Sultan. See Singleton, Op cit.

[40] Singleton, Op cit., p. 28.

[41] See Pavlowitch, *Yugoslavia* (London: Ernest Ben Limited, 1971), p. 31.

[42] Singleton, Op cit., p. 31.

[43] Quicherat, J.E.J., *Process de condemnation et de rehabilitation de Jeanne d'Arc*, in: Hastings, Op cit., p. 98.

[44] Donia, *el al*, Op cit., pp. 20-21.

[45] Ibid., p. 25.

[46] Singleton, Op cit., p. 23.

[47] Singleton, Op cit., p. 23.

[48] See Hastings, Adrian, *The Construction of Nationhood* (Cambridge: Cambridge University Press, 1997). Specifically chapter 2 "England as prototype".

[49] Interestingly the Greeks, Serbs and Bulgarians all claim Cyril and Methodius as one of their own.

[50] Clark, Samuel, *State and Status* (Montreal and Kingston: McGill-Queen's University Press, 1995), p. 129.

[51] Ibid., p. 145.

[52] This same form of social upheaval occurred during the Tito era in BiH, as the poorly educated Muslim artisan classes were rapidly transformed into a literate working class. Therefore young Muslims graduates and professions were able to articulate the needs and requirements of their community for the first time causing a degree of social unrest particularly in Sarajevo. See Glenny, Misha, *The Fall of Yugoslavia* (Harmondsworth: Penguin Books, 1992).

[53] Jelavich, 1983, Op cit., p. 165.

[54] Army of the Ottoman Sultan.

[55] Singleton, Op cit., p. 75.

[56] Pavlowitch, Op cit., p. 40.

[57] The Serbs were crushed again at the hands of the Turks in 1813. However they rose again in 1815 under Milosh Obrenovich and this time they achieved success. By 1830 the liberated territory had been recognised by the sultan as an autonomous principality, covering 38,000 square kilometres with a population of just over 700,000.

[58] Singleton, Op cit., p. 89.

[59] The education system under the Tudor dynasty (1485-1603) was one effective method of achieving a distinct view of English history and Englishness. See Cressy, David, *Education in Tudor and Stuart England* (London: Edward Arnold, 1975).

[60] Jelavich, 1983, Op cit., p. 301.

[61] Donia, *et al*, Op cit., p. 61.

[62] Ibid., p. 63.

[63] Ibid., p. 70.

[64] The abolition of serfdom under Austrian administration was little more than the legal acknowledgement of what the peasants had *already* achieved by way of revolt. Peasants became owners of the plots they had tilled, but the gentry received compensation and kept the remaining lands, which allowed estates and the powerful aristocracy to survive.

[65] Singleton, Op cit., p. 102.

Chapter 4
Dayton's Prodigy: A Construction of Necessity

Introduction

As outlined in the previous chapter the seeds of national sentiment had developed in Serbia, Croatia and Bosnia principally because of alterations in the character of sovereignty. The sentiment of nationalism continued to prevent the development of pan-Slavic brotherhood. Royal Yugoslavia and Tito's Yugoslavia failed to quell the essence of such national sentiment. The death of Marshal Josip Tito in May 1981 certainly represented a watershed insofar as the one unifying force that diverted attention away from nationalism was now gone. However, the death of Yugoslavia in reality was *not* brought about by major sporadic political events, such as the death of Tito, but had its roots in much more subtle and indeed historical political occurrences. Ethno-national sectarianism had been allowed to fester for many years and the national elections between April and December 1990 finally accommodated the manifestation of such ethnic division. As reported in *Yugoslav Life* in March of 1990, there were "new parties appearing almost daily and there may well be nearly 100 by the end of the year. Almost all parties registered so far are nationalistic in name and even more so in nature."[1]

The extent of the ethno-national character in the Balkans was vividly displayed in 1987 when Slobodan Milosevic nullified the autonomy of Kosovo and Vojvodina, although Kosovo was constituted by 90% ethnic Albanian and Vojvodina had a large Hungarian minority. "In 1990, the government of the Croatian Republic issued new regulations defining its 600,000 Serbs (almost 12 percent of Croatia's 4.7 million population...), as a "minority" rather than as a "constituent nationality..."[2] From that point forward there was little chance of a peaceful solution to the conflict. Increasingly, the Serbian leader, Milosevic, promoted the policy of "Greater Serbia".

Finally, when serious fighting broke out, the practical question for Western governments was, how could they act to end the conflict?

The seeds of hate were germinating, as was symbolised on the 28 June 1989 when several hundred thousand Serbs assembled at the battlefield site of Gazimestan, outside the Kosovar capital, Pristina, to celebrate the six-hundredth anniversary of the Battle of Kosovo. Slobodan Milosevic exploited this symbolic occasion so as to catalyse the growing sense of animosity between Serbs and non-Serbs. Milosevic exclaimed to the Serb crowd (assembled to pay homage to the bones of Prince Lazar, who died *heroically* at the battle of Kosovo) "we are again engaged in battles and quarrels. They are not armed battles, but this cannot be excluded yet."[3] Within the space of two years Bosnia was engaged in the most horrific European armed struggle since World War Two.

A growing sense of animosity, the development of ethno-national political parties and the augmentation of ethnic identity vividly displayed that the ethos of "brotherhood and Unity" had firmly been replaced by nationalistic hatred. Bosnia and in particular its capital Sarajevo, for so long the hub of assimilation and multiculturalism, fell victim to nationalism.

Bosnia's Unique Character

Bosnia was to become the hub of national sentiment in the early 1990s in the Balkans. The development of distinctiveness in present day Bosnia and Herzegovina was conditioned by both cultural and religious imperialism, as outlined in the previous chapter. Bogomil infiltration, Hungarian colonisation and Franciscan missionary conversions were some of the principal historical events that conditioned the Bosnian character. However the Ottoman invasion (battle of Mohacs 1526) was a defining moment in the development of the distinctive Bosnian character, as it brought the Islamic faith and *millet* system to Bosnia. With the infiltration of the Ottomans into Bosnia, there were now four religious communities in the region. There were Orthodox Bosnians who had been won over to the Orthodox faith between the ninth and eleventh century, when much of Bosnia was incorporated into the medieval Kingdom of Serbia. Some Bosnians were Catholic, as the Croatian Kingdom had also at times stretched into the lands of Bosnia, added to that, after 1342 the Franciscan Vicariate of Bosnia was established and converted many Bosnians to the Catholic faith. The legendary kingdom of Ban Kulin (1180-1204) saw the growth of Bogomilism (most Bogomils accepted the Islamic faith after the infiltration of the Ottomans). Finally, the Ottomans brought Islam to

Bosnia. Most significantly, the Ottomans introduced the *millet* system,[4] which institutionalised and allowed the expression of both the Catholic and Orthodox traditions in Bosnia. The *millet* system allowed all three religions to survive in the region, and right up until the present day an Orthodox church, Catholic cathedral and Islamic Mosque stand side by side in central Sarajevo.

A region such as Bosnia, based upon such religious and cultural diversity, was unquestionably vulnerable to divisive nationalism. The vulnerability became all the more intense because of the dire state of the economy from the 1970s onwards. "The Achilles heel of all Europe's communist states was the economy. Wealthy states do not break up in civil war and prosperous regimes are not toppled by revolution."[5] The communist Yugoslav state, particularly in the later years of Tito's reign had lost any incentive to reform, due to the cushion of western aid it received. The old revolutionary ideals had faded and were replaced by bureaucracy and rhetoric. The country's foreign debt rocketed from under \$3.5 billion in 1973 to more than \$ 20.5 billion in 1981.

> *Per capita* income in Slovenia, the wealthiest republic, was about three times that of Kosovo, the poorest unit, in 1945 but six times as great by the 1980s. At the same time, Yugoslavia's universities began churning out graduates in the backward republics. While their level of education led to high expectations, these were expectations that could never be fulfilled in a shrinking job market. It was a long-term recipe for disaster.[6]

Added to that the loans dried up in the early 1980s and it was now time to begin repaying the colossal national debt. After the death of Tito in 1980, Yugoslavia was faced with mounting economic problems.

> As in the royal Yugoslav era and earlier in the socialist period, Bosnians from all three major national groups supported the preservation of Yugoslavia against the forces of division and fragmentation. Those forces, [particularly mounting economic problems] however, swirled ominously around Bosnia throughout the 1980s and increasingly threatened the very existence of the Yugoslav federation.[7]

Social forces, predominantly in the form of economic crisis, created an environment fertile to nationalist rhetoric. Bosnia's industrial sector was faced with serious challenges and outside competitiveness. Industrial strikes became more common in the 1980s and inflation soared. As a reflection of the growing sectarianism, in July and August 1983, thirteen Bosnian Muslims were tried in a Sarajevo district court, accused of conspiring to transform Bosnia into an *Islamistan.* Alija Izetbegovic, who became president of Bosnia in 1992, was one of those imprisoned. One year later, Bosnian Serb Vojislav Seselj was tried for stating in an article that Bosnia should be partitioned between Croatia and Serbia, and that Montenegro be merged with Serbia. It is evident therefore that the seeds of nationalism had already begun to fester in the Bosnian psyche. Although for a time Markovic's administration attempted to resolve the economic crisis, it was too little too late. It is clear that economic deprivation and disparity fuelled the fires of nationalism. However, its not enough to assume that economic growth can resolve the global wars of nationalism. Firstly, economic growth will not necessarily resolve economic disparity between nations. Secondly, there are other forms of alienation, in addition to economic, which must be resolved if the national sentiment is to be watered-down.

The Process of Disintegration

In 1990, with the continued nationalistic rhetoric and action of Milosevic and the Serbian Socialist Party and the Croatian Democratic Union, under Tudjman, the Muslims of Bosnian felt vulnerable. In May 1990, the Bosnian Muslims in response to such vulnerability found ethno-nationalist political representation in a new nationalist political party, the Party of Democratic Action (SDA).

> Placed between the hammer and the anvil of Serbian and Croatian nationalism, the Bosnian Muslims reacted in two different ways: they strengthened their own Muslim nationalism by giving greater emphasis to the most distinctive thing about it, its religious component, and they also emphasised that they stood for the preservation of Bosnia's character as a multi-national, multi-religious republic.[8]

Of course these two principles clearly opposed one another and as the war progressed the latter principle capitulated due to the ferocity with which the former was articulated. With the dissolution of the League of the Communists of Yugoslavia (LCY), multiparty elections took place in each of the six Yugoslav republics in 1990. The Bosnian elections were held in November and manifested the extent of ethno-national awareness in the region. In fact ethnically based parties won 86% of the 240 seats in the Bosnian Assembly. On January 30, 1991, the Muslim Party for Democratic Action submitted a proposal for a sovereign Bosnia; the Croatians agreed with the proposal. The Serbian Democratic Party (SDS), however, wanted to remain in the Serbian-dominated Yugoslav federation. Nevertheless, in October 1991, the Muslims and Croatian parties passed a resolution demanding sovereignty for Bosnia. Meanwhile, by 1991, the Serbs had established Serb ethnic enclaves within Bosnia, "Serb Autonomous Regions" as they were named. Finally, on December 21, 1991, Bosnia's Serbs declared their own republic.

In September 1991 the local Serb SDS leadership requested that the federal army enter Bosnia to protect the enclaves from sporadic Muslim attack. In such an environment there was little chance that the SDA's call for a multi-cultural Bosnia could be attained. As the situation continually deteriorated the international community, represented at this stage by appointed negotiator, Lord Carrington, continued to believe that some form of federal style Yugoslavia could be maintained. Immediately before the outbreak of the conflict, Western European leaders wished to maintain Yugoslavia's territorial integrity and unity, in the interest of order, stability and balance of power in the Balkans. However, the EC was also forced to deal with claims of self-determination. In attempting to square this circle, the EC under the stewardship of Lord Carrington, showed itself to be limited, insofar as it failed to envisage solutions outside the realm of territorial demarcation, centralised sovereignty and spatial exclusion. The Carrington Conference proposals "essentially allowed for the creation of a new Yugoslavia modelled on the EC, with particular attention given to issues of minority rights and autonomy including a central court of appeal charged especially with the defence of those rights".[9] The plan to create a "Balkan EC" in no manner alleviated the complexities arising from the intensification in ethno-nationalism, as the development of such a structure did not create space (capable of accommodating multiple identities), but rather institutionalised the demarcation of space. Serbia rejected the settlement and indeed Croatia was also dubious regarding the proposals. Whilst the proposals accepted self-determination they also attempted to introduce rights for minorities within states, in this way administering a local anaesthetic against the ills of self-determination. The Serbs felt that their minorities could not be protected outside the Serbian nation state, whilst the Croats were unwilling to accept limits on its ability to protect and promote Croatian interests within their own nation state, even where these trampled on the rights of others. The failure of the EU to construct a post-territorial solution resulted in the failure of Carrington's initiative. A post-territorial proposal would rather attempt to create space so as to accommodate all identities, through a process whereby territory is open to the influence of multiple dispersed sovereignties, as outlined in chapter two. After Croatia had been accepted as a sovereign nation state on 15

January 1992, following a peace settlement brokered by UN representative Cyrus Vance, there was little chance of maintaining the federal Yugoslav structure. On the 29 February and 1 March 1992, a referendum was held in Bosnia. Although the SDS forbade Serbs from voting in the referendum, roughly 64% of the population voted nevertheless. On the ballot paper Bosnians were asked: "Are you in favour of a sovereign and independent Bosnia and Herzegovina, a state of equal citizens and nations of Muslims, Serbs, Croats and others who live in it?"[10] The clear majority voted 'yes'. On 6 April 1992 Bosnia was recognised as an independent state by the EC; the war had now truly begun.

Three into One Won't Go

"Bosnia could never be a state, they claimed, because it contained three different nationalities; the first of these claims begged the question of whether only nation-states are viable states."[11] Although it did contain three different nationalities, or more accurately one nationality divided by conquest into three different religions, there is no reason why previously multi-ethnic, multi-cultural Bosnia could not respond to such challenges.

Bosnia had never been a hot bed of fervent nationalism, as most conflict and rebellion in the past was based upon economic issues rather than any form of ethno-nationalism. Conflict between local Muslim elite and the peoples of Bosnia in the past had been fuelled by social and economic factors. However, just as in the past, outside forces with powerful ambition attempted to take advantage of Bosnia.[12] The Croatian nationalists, represented by Tudjman and the HDZ hoped to annex much of western Herzegovina, while Serb nationalists, led by Milosevic's SDS, regarded Bosnia as part of Serbia. The Serb paramilitary forces arrived in the town of Bijeljina on the first days of April under the control of the notorious warlord Arkan. Serb atrocities against Muslims began in earnest from this point onwards. The Yugoslav federal army practically became the tool of Serb aggression, and obviously Muslim retaliation was meek and sporadic given both the strength of the Yugoslav army forces and the relative inexperience and weakness of Muslim militias.

Ironically, but not surprisingly, knowing that outside actors have continually over time shaped Bosnia's history, the Croats became the main opposition to Serb aggression in the early stages of the war. In western Herzegovina the local Croats had made some preparations, and had been joined by men from the Croatian paramilitary force. In response to the war, the UN assessed the consequences of the war more than the causes. "The actions of the UN and its member states, although numerous and costly, were therefore more effective in assuaging Western consciences than in providing a lasting solution to the crisis."[13] In late October 1992 the EC and the UN negotiators, Lord Owen and Cyrus Vance, produced the first detailed proposal for a political settlement. The merits of the Vance-Owen plan were its insistence that refugees should be allowed to return to their homes throughout Bosnia, and its provisions that the cantons corresponding to Serb occupied areas would not be connected on the map in such a way as to make it easy for them to join Serbian territory.[14] *Real Politik* mitigated against the realisation of this plan, as there was no chance that Serb controlled cantons would allow the return of Muslim or Croat refugees; secondly Serbs controlled the cantons neighbouring the Serbian state thereby rendering the plan unworkable. The most negative result of the plan was that it formally ethnically labeled cantons and invariably brought Muslim and Croat militia into clashes with one another over specific territories. By early April 1993 there was widespread fighting between Croats and Muslims in the area of central Bosnia. The situation was assessed on 22 May 1993 when foreign ministers, from Britain, France, Spain, Russia and the US, gathered in Washington. The threat of air strikes was dropped, and instead "safe areas" were created to protect the 2 million Muslims. Safety was to be provided by the UN, thus bringing the UN into the war as an actor perceived by Croats and Serbs as pro-Muslim. With the threat of air strikes having been dropped, Muslims, even those within the jurisdiction of "safe areas", were in grave danger.

After the rejection of the Vance-Owen plan by the Serbs, the international community capitulated to the forces of realist power politics by accepting alterations created by way of military conquest. A new plan, drawn up by Lord Owen and the former Norwegian Foreign Minister Thorvald Stoltenberg, gave the Serbs 53 per cent of the Bosnian territory, the Muslims 30 per cent and the Croats 17 per cent. In essence what was being proposed was the creation of three ethnically homogenous "sovereign nation states". All parties failed to agree on territorial distribution and percentages, as it became clear, considering that the Serbs received 53 per cent of the territory in the plan, that aggression was a worthwhile and fruitful exercise. The situation reached such an abyss in the winter of 93-94 that the UN mission, UNPROFOR, considered pulling out and conceding failure. There are three fundamental reasons why the school of thought that promotes the idea of Bosnia being partitioned into three sovereign nation states is grossly wrong. Firstly, to do so would explicitly validate the process of ethic cleansing which had taken place. It would also have shown ethnic cleansing to be both a successful tactic and very much a political maneuver. Secondly, minorities living within sovereign nation states would be forced to either assimilate or move, thus destroying the former multi-ethnic character of Bosnia. Thirdly, deciding on the demarcation of borders between the three states would engender great fratricidal conflict, as the multi-ethnic character of Bosnia does not facilitate demarcation in line with ethnicity.

Reaction to the Mortar Shell Attack

The ethos of the international community was to change drastically in 1994, after a mortar shell landed in a busy Sarajevo marketplace, killing sixty-eight people and wounding two hundred others. "Although the attack was only one of hundreds that had killed and maimed civilians since the war began, the concentrated and highly publicised slaughter crossed an imaginary threshold of the world's toleration for violence."[15] NATO subsequently issued an ultimatum to the Serbs, the French began to promote NATO air strikes and the Americans became more involved in the war.[16]

Another significant turning point in the war was the ending of the Croat-Muslim war in central Bosnia. Formal agreement was signed creating a federation based upon cantons between Croats and Muslims within Bosnia.[17] The vital achievement of this agreement was to see the Muslims and Croats fighting together against the Serbs from this point onwards. In May of 1994 a Contact Group, consisting of Britain, France, Germany, Russia and America, forwarded the idea of preserving the integrity of the Republic of Bosnia and Herzegovina, by territorially dividing the country into two halves, 51 per cent of the territory to the newly formed Croat-Muslim federation and 49 per cent to the Serbs. The Bosnian Serbs rejected the plan and fighting continued amidst a myriad of cease-fires. During May 1995 a crisis suddenly arose, as NATO was finally granted permission by the UN to respond with air strikes to a Serb bombardment of Sarajevo.

This strong action signalled a change of mindset on behalf of the international community, it was time to get serious about Bosnia. However, such assertive action was also marred with unassertiveness and naivete, symbolised by the fall of Srebrenica on 11 July 1995. On July 6, Mladic's forces began shelling Srebrenica. On July 10 they invaded the town and took the Dutch peacekeepers hostage. The next day Mladic entered Srebrenica and announced, "finally, after the rebellion of the Dahijas, the time has come to take revenge on the Turks of this region". This was a direct reference to the rebellion of 1804 that was brutally crushed by the

Ottomans.[18] Mladic's remarks manifest the use and abuse of history in pursuing war objectives.

To End a War

After a Serb mortar attack on a Sarajevo market on 28 August 1995, which killed 37 people and wounded 88, the UN and NATO issued an ultimatum to General Mladic to remove his artillery from Sarajevo. When he refused NATO bombing began in earnest. With the continuing NATO air raids, an American-led diplomatic mission attempted to flesh out a peace plan based upon the previous contact group plan. This peace mission finally culminated with a three week long session at a US air force base in Dayton, Ohio, where *the Dayton Peace Accord* was hammered out by an American negotiating team, led by Richard Holbrooke, Milosevic, representing the Bosnian Serbs, Tudjman representing the Croats and Izetbegovic representing the Muslims.

The Dayton agreement maintained the 51:49 per cent division between the Muslim-Croat Federation and the Serb republic, developed previously by the multi-national contact group. It also contained a new constitution, human rights protection mechanisms, right of return for refugees and displaced persons, the reconstruction of the economy and a plan for the deployment of an international force, under NATO leadership, of 60,000 troops to supervise the cessation of hostilities. *The Dayton Peace Accord* attempted to "create two functioning levels of government: a central government, with its capital in Sarajevo; and two regional entities, one a functioning Croat-Muslim Federation, the other the existing Bosnian Serb entity, but minus any claims to sovereignty".[19] It was agreed that the Federation would turn responsibility for certain functions, such as foreign affairs, over to the new central government, which would include Muslims, Serbs and Croats. In turn, local matters such as police, education, and internal security would be assigned to each of the entities, namely the Federation and Republika Srpska (RS).

The consequences of the war in Bosnia and Herzegovina are vast and incalculable, but it is generally estimated that 258,000 inhabitants died or are missing.[20] Apart from those who died and are missing the war created 1,282,000 Internally Displaced Persons (DP's) and there were 1.2 million refugees from BiH at the end of the war. "Indirect effects, such as the destruction of the governance system, the interruption of reconstruction, education and development of technology, as well as "brain drain", although immeasurable, are undoubtedly colossal."[21]

The War is Over: Negotiating a Peace Settlement

For some the negotiation of a peace settlement represented the culmination of international peace efforts in Bosnia between 1992 and 1995, including efforts of Lord Carrington, Lord Owen and Cyrus Vance, Lord Owen and Thorvald Stoltenberg, and others including UNPROFOR forces and the UN Secretary General. However, in some respects the Dayton agreement was brought to bare by the lack of progress of these previous, often disjointed, peace attempts.

A clear understanding of the objectives of *the Dayton Peace Accord* is difficult to identify from the *Accord* itself. Its architect, Richard Holbrooke, writing in September 1999 claims that: "the central principal of the 1995 Dayton peace agreement (was) a single, multiethnic country".[22] It is clear that the different parties to the agreement had different objectives for it. These objectives cover a wide range of targets. William Perry's optimistic, "one year will be sufficient to break the cycle of violence in Bosnia" which he broke down into "four to six months to enforce a truce and disarmament, and another six months to create a secure environment",[23] contrasts with Holbrooke's own more limited initial objectives "to end a war". Carl Bildt focused on the democratisation and civil administration objectives of the *Accord* and saw these as prime objectives, while Admiral Leighton Smith viewed his objectives for IFOR through a very blinkered periscope.[24] The Bosnian Serbs saw Dayton as giving them the partition of Bosnia that they had fought for. The Bosnian Muslims viewed the objectives of Dayton with suspicion, pessimism and in some cases with a deep sense of injustice. These feelings were expressed clearly by Alija Izetbegovic in his first public response to the successful conclusion of the Dayton negotiations.[25]

The Dayton Political Structure

The political structure of Bosnia and Herzegovina[26] is outlined principally in annex IV of the *Dayton Peace Accord*. Bosnia and Herzegovina has a system of governance, over which a foreign *High Representative* has over-riding authority. It includes a Troika, *rotating Presidency*, with a *Council of Ministers* and a *bicameral Assembly*, none of which exercise effective national authority over two separate and different types of government at entity level. These two entities preside over separate non-sovereign states. *The Federation of Bosnia and Herzegovina*, one of these entities, has two *de facto* armies, two divided communities and is governed by an appointed

Entity Presidency, a bicameral *Parliamentary Assembly* and, at local level, has *Cantonal* and *Municipal* assemblies. The other entity, *Republika Srpska*, has an elected *Presidency*, an elected *National Assembly* and *Municipal Assemblies.*[27]

As is evident from appendix 2 and 3, the government structure of Bosnia and Herzegovina (BiH) is a multi-layered type of government. While the official functions of the Peace Implementation Council and the High Representative are unclear in the context of both Bosnian and International law, the authority exercised by the OHR is considerable. In practice the OHR promotes the effective progress and accommodation in the nine layers of governmental institutions. Layer one is a nine-member Constitutional Court, with four members appointed by the Federation House of Representatives and two appointed by the Republika Srpska national assembly. The European Court of Human Rights appoints the remaining three members. Layer two, is a loose central government, with little real power. The presidency of the central government consists of three directly elected rotating presidents. Layer three forms the executive branch of the central government. The executive branch, namely the council of ministers, are nominated by the BiH Presidency, approved by the BiH House of Representatives and by the UN appointed High Representative. Layer four consists of a bicameral Bosnia and Herzegovina Parliamentary Assembly, consisting of the Bosnia and Herzegovina House of Representatives (Elected) and the Bosnia and Herzegovina House of People (Selected). Layer five consists of the presidency of the Croat/Muslim Federation (dual, rotating, selected presidents), and Republika Srpska (single, elected president). Below layer five, the systems of governance diverge, becoming more complicated. At layer six, the Croat/Muslim Federation, duplicates layer four of the central government with an elected BiH House of Representatives and a selected BiH House of Peoples. In Republika Srpska, there is only one house of parliament, namely the RS national assembly. Layer seven in the federation, contains a further anomaly, in that there is a separate layer of ten elected Cantonal assemblies. There are no corresponding cantonal assemblies in Republika Srpska. The elected municipal assemblies in both the federation and RS form the eight layer of governance. Finally, the citizens of BiH form the ninth layer, as the voters who directly or indirectly elect and maintain the institutional structures.

The Principal Articles of the Accord

The leaders of the three national governments of Serbia, Croatia and Bosnia signed the principal articles of the *Accord*. The signing of the *Accord*, which took place officially in Paris on December 14 1995, brought the following stipulations into effect. Serbia, Croatia and Bosnia were to recognise each other as sovereign states and renounce the use of force against each other.

- The parties were to accept implementation of the military and stabilisation provisions of the agreement, by the NATO led Implementation Force (IFOR); subsequently to become (SFOR) in 1997.
- Accept agreed boundaries between the Federation of BiH and Rebublika Srpska.
- Endorse the election programme for BiH.
- Endorse the Constitution of BiH.
- Endorse the agreement of arbitration, and commissions on human rights, refugees and Displaced Persons (DPs), national monuments and public corporations.
- Co-operate with the investigation and prosecution of war crimes and human rights violation.
- Comply and co-operate with the various articles and annexes to the Accord.

The Dayton Peace Accord and the People Factor

The Dayton Peace Accord can be enforced by the presence and threat of NATO armed force, just as the Ottoman Empire and Tito's regime enforced their particular forms of rule. However for democracy to take hold in Bosnia, using the Dayton formula, the people of Bosnia must perceive Dayton as the ultimate step towards both peace and justice. There are many issues arising out of the *Accord* that are perceived as unjust.

From a Bosnian Muslim point of view there are two serious issues of justice. The crimes committed against the Muslim community, mainly by Serbs and Bosnian Serbs, have not been addressed or even adequately acknowledged by the international community. The massacres, gross human rights abuses and ethnic cleansing that occurred in the Muslim areas of Srebrenica and Prijador, for example, and the complacency of the international community in failing to prevent these atrocities, cannot be forgotten by the present generations of Bosnian Muslims. Another major issue of injustice to the Bosnian Muslim community is the terms of the Dayton settlement which awarded 49% of the territory to the Bosnian Serbs and 51% to the combined Croat/Muslim federation; these two entities being demarcated by a pseudo-border, namely the Inter-Entity Boundary Line (IEBL). If the pre-war population statistics are analysed the injustice of this settlement becomes evident. The 1991 Yugoslav census of population showed that the Bosnian people declared themselves to be as follows:

Muslim	43.7%
Serb	31.4%
Croat	17.3%
Yugoslav	5.5%
Other	2.1%

Therefore by no juggling of mathematics could this divide be considered just or equitable. From these figures it would seem almost as it the Bosnian Serbs had "won the war". However, what is often forgotten is the fact that up to 90,000 Bosnian Serbs were killed in the war, and many Bosnian Serbs have been ethnically cleansed from Muslim and Croat areas of Bosnia. While it can be argued that the Serbs bear responsibility for their own misfortune, this applies more at a political leadership level than at individual or local community levels. Very many innocent Serbs have been victims of the Bosnian war, and the Serb community, as a whole, feel victimised by the international community.

It is certainly a reality that the Croats carried out some of the worst atrocities in the war. For example, on 16 April 1993, over 100 Muslim villagers were massacred by Croat HVO forces in the village of Ahmici near Vitez in Central Bosnia.[28] Nevertheless, certain Croats within BiH feel aggrieved, as they did not gain entity status, whereas the Bosnian Serbs did. Particularly in Canton 7, in the Mostar region of western BiH, many ethno-nationalist Croats hoped to attain Croat entity status. The system of government imposed by Dayton, effectively dilutes the power and responsibilities of central government. However, there is a real fear that such a dis-aggregation of power away from the centre may allow the national assembly in Republika Srpska to take on nation state status, thereby alienating the Muslims and Croats living in, or wishing to return, to the entity.[29] Considering that there is no cantonal level of governance in Republika Srpska, there is indeed a very real threat that the Serb dominated national assembly may alienate the Muslim and Croat minorities. It can strongly be argued that Dayton should have concentrated to a larger extent upon preventing one community from dominating either of the other two.

If a lasting peace is to be created in BiH, these are some of the principal issues of justice and equality that must be addressed, even at this stage, six years after the conflict. Within the next chapter, an analysis is undertaken as to how such issues of justice and equality can be strengthened and maintained.

The International Actors: Who is in Charge?

The initial task of taking charge, enforcing a cease-fire, establishing peace, separation of forces and stabilisation of the security and military situation fell to the NATO (US-led) *IFOR Implementation Force*. In the five years since NATO forces intervened in Bosnia, no NATO soldiers have been killed in military action. In fact stabilisation of the security and military situations were achieved sooner than expected by IFOR. However, problems arose regarding the implementation of other aspects of Dayton. Initial IFOR reservations had the effect of almost crippling the implementation of the *Dayton Accord*, especially in dealing with such issues as the arrest of war criminals and the return of refugees and Displaced Persons across inter-ethnic boundaries. The failure of IFOR to support the return of refugees to their original locations had a series of knock on effects. In many areas, refugees and DP's have occupied the homes of expelled refugees and displaced persons from other communities. This applies to all three communities in both entities. The longer this situation is allowed to continue, the more entrenched the DP's become in their temporary homes, and the more likely they are to resist, by force if necessary, the return of the original occupants.

The Office of the High Representative (OHR) The OHR, led by Carl Bildt from 1995 to 1997; Carlos Westendorp 1997 to 1999 and led now by High Representative Wolfgang Petritish, is responsible for the civil implementation of the *Accord*. As to whom the High Representative is responsible to, or represents, is difficult to establish. While the first High Representative Carl Bildt had worked with the EU, as EU co-chairman of the International Conference on Former Yugoslavia in 1995, he makes it clear that the OHR is in no way related to the EU.[30] He also makes the point that he was not under the authority of the UN Secretary General, even though the UN nominated him. The OHR acts almost like a "father figure" intervening when absolutely necessary so as to promote the civil implementation of the *Accord*. It is important that such intervention is firstly rare, so as to limit the constellation of dependency syndrome. Secondly such intervention should promote an ethos of multiculturalism, thus catalysing co-operation between all peoples in the long term.

The Organisation for Security and Co-operation in Europe (OSCE) The OSCE was given the vital task of preparing for and organising elections in Bosnia. The timetable set for elections had been decided at Dayton, stipulating that elections should take place no later than nine months after the signing of the *Accord*. The time scale meant that election preparations had to be rushed, but more seriously, it did not allow time for the constellation of grass-roots democratic developments. This gave the nationalist parties in each community, who in all three cases already controlled the limited administration, media and financial resources, an unstoppable electoral advantage. The results of the national and local elections merely reflected the ethnic divisions within BiH, with each ethnic group voting steadfastly for their own ethno-nationalist candidate. The election results therefore gave the Serb SDS, Croat HDZ and Muslim SDA, a legitimate power base that they would use to further their own ends at the expense of implementing Dayton in the spirit of co-operation and flexibility necessary, if the process of democratisation was to succeed.

Humanitarian and Developmental Organisations BiH is one of the biggest beneficiaries of international assistance in various fields since the signing of the GFAP. The significance of humanitarian and developmental organisations cannot be overstated, as they have been a fundamental variable in promoting reconciliation. Even though the population of BiH would have had great difficulty in "normalising" life after the war, were it not for international assistance, care must be taken nevertheless that foreign aid does not nurture a dependency syndrome. It is necessary therefore that international assistance be aimed towards the creation of local capacity building.[31] Up to now, the international community has concentrated on taking over the traditional role of the state in providing for the needs of the people. The international community are now attempting to exit this "dependency crisis" through the development of local capacity building. This will create a constructive consciousness amongst the peoples of BiH, making them mould and take responsibility for their future.

The European Community Humanitarian Office (ECHO), one such functionalist body promoting local capacity building, was set up in 1992, when the European Union decided on a new initiative to assist victims of the conflict in Former Yugoslavia. At first, the aim was to save lives and to ensure survival. Humanitarian operations focused on providing medical aid, food, clothing and hygienic items. As the situation evolved, it became clear ECHO needed to be closer to the ground and to its implementing partners, namely NGO's. Therefore, in 1996 ECHO opened an office in Sarajevo and established a working network in BiH. At its height ECHO employed 45 full time staff in the network, involving 10 international staff and 35 local employees.[32] ECHO has two main objectives in BiH, the first one is to provide essential assistance to those in need, as large-scale displacement within the region is still causing serious humanitarian, social, economical and political difficulties. Developing human resources and strengthening management and institutions is ECHO's second objective. In this regard they hope to transfer competence and capacity to local indigenous institutions, so called capacity building.

SFOR – Stabilisation Phase A major change in U.S. policy on Bosnia was indicated on 20 December 1997 when, "President Clinton held a news conference in which he announced that the United States would keep its troops in Bosnia past the original June 1998 deadline".[33] SFOR under new leadership invigorated the implementation process and from mid-1997 onwards the process of democratisation began in earnest. Richard Halbrooke neatly sums up the extent to which the process of democratisation had developed since the signing of the Accord on a trip to Sarajevo in August 1997. "…[A]bout one year behind where we should be… The good news in Sarajevo was that the joint institutions actually existed; the bad news was that they barely functioned."[34]

The Others et al The above-mentioned are just some of the main international agencies involved in post-Dayton Bosnia. In addition there are others, too numerous to analyse here, including the United Nations, governments of each of the countries that involved themselves in Bosnia, and myriad humanitarian and political NGO's. The combined impacts of all these agents represent the influence of the international community on Bosnia, and on its prospects for democracy.

Life after Dayton

The *Dayton Peace Accord* may have ended the war, but did not necessarily create peace. The Serbs in Republika Srpska felt aggrieved, as they had lost Sarajevo, and in its place had gained large spans of destitute land. Added to that, Serbs were continually fleeing the federation, in fear of both Muslim/Croat and Serb aggression. Muslims and Croats felt they had lost the war as well, as RS had gained 49% of the territory and received entity status. Certainly many Serbs wanted to remain or return to Sarajevo. However, they found it difficult to accept Muslim rule. For example, the RS vice-president Biljana Plavsic, on meeting Carl Bildt for the first time in 1995, urged him to facilitate Serbs in Sarajevo, as it was important that Serbs maintain links with Sarajevo. Added to that, on a practical note, Banja Luka, the RS capital was unable to take care of any more Serb refugees fleeing the federation.[35] However, the creation of a multi-ethnic Sarajevo, as a symbol of the future for the whole of Bosnian was an enormous task. Initial endeavours proved fruitless, as the degree of hostility was palpable.[36] The creation of common institutions, even on a symbolic level, would be a necessary prerequisite, in order to create a multi-ethnic character and sense of trust between the communities. Multi-ethnic common institutions residing in Sarajevo would have the effect of linking the RS with Sarajevo and the Federation, thus affording Serbs living in the Federation some form of representation. On another level, it would help reduce the significance of the entity status ascribed to RS, and in this manner would reduce the significance of the Inter Entity Boundary Line. However, common institutions could not be created until elections had been held. All parties had agreed at Dayton to hold the elections early. "For the Serbs, elections were a way to sanction status quo [to legitimise the serbianisation of RS], while for the Muslims they were a way to roll everything back to the pre-war status [through "out of country voting" and ability to vote in pre-war constituencies]."[37]

Because of technical, logistical and blatant attempts by nationalist political parties to influence the results of election, local elections were postponed until spring 1997. National elections went ahead on 14 September 1996. In RS the main political parties were the SDS, formerly chaired by Radovan Karadzic and excessively nationalist. The SMP, the Union for Peace and Progress, was a sister party of Milosevic's Socialist party in Serbia. It was evident that they were not going to enjoy much success, as many Bosnian Serbs regarded Milosevic as a traitor, after the Dayton talks. In the Federation, the campaign was more intense in the Muslim controlled areas as there were several parties challenging the dominant Muslim SDA political party. Hasis Silajdzic and his Pro-Bosnia party had decided to directly challenge the SDA and Izetbegovic. In addition, there were also the moderate Social Democratic Party, headed by Zlatko Lagumdzija, and the attempt to create a more explicitly multi-ethnic Joint List electoral system. In the climate of fervent nationalism the slogan of the SDA 'our own faith, our own country', was bound to succeed. In the Croat districts the same applied, and indeed the ruling HDZ party's dominance was even clearer, as they had access to Zagreb based propaganda sources.

It had been an election dominated far more by fears coming out of the past than by hopes for a better future; and therefore voters voted clearly along ethno-nationalist lines. In elections to the common parliamentary assembly, for example, in which the Federation voted for twenty-eight seats and the Republika Srpska voted for fourteen, the SDA won nineteen seats, the SDS nine and the HDZ three, with the remainder going to smaller parties. Evidently the ethno-national political parties who fought the war continued to maintain their power base in the initial post-war environment. Following the elections, it was the aim of High Representative Bildt to create the common institutions by the end of 1996 so as to initiate the process of civil implementation. This process took a great deal of patience and tenacity but was nevertheless put in place by the end of 1996.

The Anomaly of Brcko

The creation of common institutions, with jurisdiction over the two entities, got off to a slow and fragile start in 1997. The complexity of the situation was exacerbated by the fact that the district of Brcko had been placed under international mandate in the Dayton agreement (GFA, 1995, Annex 1-B. par. 2). A week before the mandate expired in December 1996, it was decided that the mandate be extended. Robert Owen, the international arbiter, "had not been convinced that any of the three candidates [the Federation, Republika Srpska, or the joint Bosnian institutions] were sufficiently stabilised to take on the situation".[38] In order to strengthen local democratic institutions the Arbitration tribunal, under Owen, issued a ruling on 14 April 1997 outlining nine key factors to be included in the work of the Brcko supervisor, Robert Farrand, appointed by the OHR.[39] Finally on March 5th 1999 the arbitration tribunal issued a Final Award creating the special autonomous district of Brcko. The district of Brcko has attempted since its inception to deliver *a working peace system*. Such attempts will be outlined in chapter five. However, it is significant to note that the Brcko arbitration ruling focused to a greater extent upon governance of the district, rather than demarcation of territory. In this sense, the arbitration ruling reflects a determination to create a post-territorial solution.

The Democratisation of Bosnia

The creation and development of multi-ethnic administrations formed at all levels is a most positive progression towards democratisation. However, the success of political parties that appeal *only* to one ethnic group is a central barrier to democratisation and the Dayton process. Multi-ethnic political parties have found it exceedingly difficult to garner support among the Bosnian electorate (the April 2000 municipal elections being the exception). In the September 1998 State and entity elections, for example, the Muslim SDA and the Croat HDZ secured substantial majorities, while the Serb SDS remains the largest party in RS. In fact the hard line Serb nationalist parties out-polled the moderate Serb nationalist coalition, led by Biljana Plavsic, who lost out to Serb Radical party representative Nikola Poplasen for the RS presidency.

The prominence of multi-ethnic parties has indeed prevented the advancement of civil society. As exclaimed by former High Representative Westendorp,

> ...there are many obstacles towards the democratisation process. It is essentially the lack of a really structured civilian society...the presence of mono-ethnic parties, which do not really contribute to the pluralistic system. There is a democratic system in the sense that there are democratic elections, but the results of the elections is that they give the advantage to one ethnic group over another. This is only a continuation of the war with other means. So in order to develop democratisation, it is necessary to implant more pluralism in the political parties. It is necessary to encourage the development of multi-ethnic parties.[40]

The task of building a multi ethnic pluralist political system falls within the jurisdiction of the OSCE under annex 3. To this end the OSCE, in co-ordination with the OHR, is attempting to promote a non-national political alternative. In forwarding the non-national alternative in a bid to create civil society, the NGO sector played and continues to play a fundamental role. NGOs are destined to play an important role in the post-conflict situation as they have a vast potential for transcending the fault-lines. To this end the democratisation branch of the OSCE supports them. The international community supports the endeavour of creating a civil society by donating funds, so that NGOs have the means and funds with which to act. This approach is supported particularly by the European Union through its European Community Humanitarian Office (ECHO). "The breaking down of mental barriers, which will allow people to establish public organisations creating alternatives to solutions proposed by governments and local authorities, is a key task of the European Union and international organisations supporting NGOs in Bosnia and Herzegovina."[41] As a means of both supporting and co-ordinating the NGO sector, the OSCE established the NGO Development Programme. The programme is geared to giving these organisations a strong political voice of opposition to the dominant ethno-national political parties. The OSCE, in this regard, has supported the establishment of a Citizens Alternative Parliament and the Coalition for Return.[42] It appears that the international community have become aware that opposition to ethno national political parties and progress on refugee return are most likely to be successful if supported from "below".

Epilogue: The Road to a Working Peace

After six years of painstakingly slow success in the process of developing peace in BiH, it is time to assess and fundamentally tackle the principal factors that can deliver a working and lasting peace in the region. From an analysis of the peace implementation process outlined in the latter section of this chapter, life after Dayton appears dependent upon a number of developments, such as the positive evolution of the political structures independently from the international community. The growth in multi-ethnic pluralist political parties is also a prerequisite for future stability and inclusion. Again the sense of tangible and intangible injustice and inequality felt by large sections of all ethnicities must be fundamentally redressed. Finally, the work and endeavour of humanitarian and developmental institutions must be supported with the aim of empowering local people. The momentum of peace and reconciliation has begun in BiH, whilst commentators may feel frustrated with the pace or character of this process, it must be kept in mind that the Bosnian war was the most ferocious and barbaric European conflict since World War Two. When put in this context, the process of reconciliation appears phenomenal.

Within the next chapter a number of burning issues, which hold the key to "softening" monolithic national identity/loyalty and creating *human security* in Bosnia, are scrutinised. Using the theoretical model of dispersed horizontal and vertical sovereignty critiqued in chapter two, it is my aim to analyse how best a vertical and horizontal dispersal of sovereignty could be enhanced in post-Dayton Bosnia, so as to create space, celebrate identity and ultimately deconstruct ethno-nationalism. In addition to the use of secondary sources, I also carried out primary research. The aim of the research undertaken was to critique the extent to which the post-Dayton implementation process has succeeded in creating space and challenging monolithic identity. In tackling this question it must be seen whether the implementation process in post-Dayton Bosnia is helping to create *human-security*. The fundamental objective is to ascertain whether the institutionally decentralised governance created, is capable of presenting workable post-territorial solutions.

Notes

[1] Milosevic, B. "Political Parties", *Yugoslav Life* (Published by Tanjug News Agency) March, 1990, p. 8.

[2] Dean, Jonathan, *Ending Europe's Wars* (New York: A Twentieth Century Fund Book, 1994), p. 131.

[3] Beloff, *Tito's Flawed Legacy*, in: Malcolm, Noel, *Bosnia: A short history* (London: Macmillan Press, 1996), p. 213.

[4] For explanation of the *millet* system, see chapter three.

[5] Bennett, Christopher, *Yugoslavia's Bloody Collapse* (London: Hurst and Company, 1995), p. 67.

[6] Ibid., p. 69.

[7] Fine, John V.A. and Donia, Robert, J. *Bosnia and Hercegovina: A tradition betrayed* (London: Hurst and Company, 1994), p. 195.

[8] Malcolm, Noel, *Bosnia: A short history* (London: Macmillan, 1996), pp. 218-219.

[9] *Financial Times*, "Copy Us, EC Tells Warring Yugoslavs", November, 1991, pp. 19-20, in: Williams, John, *Legitimacy in International Relations and the Rise and Fall of Yugoslavia* (London: Macmillan Press, 1998), p. 137.

[10] Mazower, *War in Bosnia*, in: Malcolm, Noel, Op cit., p. 231.

[11] Malcolm, Noel, Op cit., p. 234.

[12] For example, subsequent to the peasant revolts in Bosnia against austerity arising from Ottoman infiltration, Great power intervention placed Bosnia under equally austere Austrian jurisdiction in 1875.

[13] Fine, John, V.A., Op cit., p. 257.

[14] See Malcolm, Noel, Op cit., pp. 247-48.

[15] Fine, John, V.A. ,and Donia, Robert, J.Op cit., p. 268.

[16] It has been suggested by Serb elements that the mortar attack was initiated by the Muslims so as to force the International Community into action. The Muslims on the other hand strongly refute the idea that they would have killed 68 of their own people for political gain.

[17] This agreement was signed on 1 March 1994 by Dr. Silajdzic, Prime Minister of the Republic of Bosnia and Herzegovina, Dr. Granic, Deputy Prime Minister of the Republic of Croatia, and Mr. Zubak, Head of the Bosnian Croat delegation. The framework agreement for the Federation provided that Bosniaks and Croats, as constituent peoples (along with others) and citizens of the Republic of Bosnia and Herzegovina, in the exercise of their sovereign rights, transform the internal structure of the territories with a majority of Bosniak and Croat population in the Republic of Bosnia and Herzegovina into the Federation, which is composed of federal units with equal rights and responsibilities. See De Rossanet, Bertrand, *Peacemaking and peacekeeping in Yugoslavia* (The Hague: Kluwer Law International, 1996), p. 60.

[18] See Holbrooke, Richard, *To end a war* (New York: Random House, 1998), p. 69.

[19] Holbrooke, Richard, Op cit., p. 241.

[20] According to the BiH Public Health Institute estimates.

[21] Independent Bureau for Humanitarian Issues, Human Development Report Bosnia and Herzegovina 1998, p. 19.

[22] Holbrooke, Richard, "In the Balkans be sure to carry on for the long haul", *International Herald Tribune*, Sept. 15, 1999, p. 6.

[23] Holbrooke, Richard, 1998. Op cit., p. 319.

[24] Holbrooke believed that Smith failed to implement the spirit of Dayton and quotes IFOR's inaction on the destruction of the Serb areas of Sarajevo in 1996 while IFOR stood idly by Ibid., p. 337.

[25] "And to my people, I say, this may not be a just peace, but it is more just than a continuation of war. In the situation as it is and in the world as it is, a better peace could not have been achieved. God is our witness that we have done everything in our power so that the extent of injustice for our people and our country would be decreased." See Holbrooke, Richard, 1998, Op cit., pp. 311-12.

[26] Bosnia had its official name changed by involuntary amputation from The Republic of Bosnia and Herzegoovina to just Bosnia and Herzegovina during the Dayton peace talks.

[27] See list of appendices, No. 2.

[28] Allcock, John, *Conflict in Former Yugoslavia, An Encyclopaedia* (Oxford: Oxford University Press, 1998), p. 2.

[29] The dominance of Serb political parties in the RS assembly would certainly validate such a fear.

[30] Bildt, Carl, *Peace Journey, The struggle for peace in Bosnia* (London: Weidenfeld and Nicholson, 1998).

[31] Presently, developmental organisations such as the European Community Humanitarian Office and USAID, are strongly pursuing a policy of local capacity building, which concentrates on equipping the local population with the knowledge and means so as to mould their future.

[32] ECHO have now relocated their main Balkan headquarters to Kosovo as from January 2000 and effectively are in the process of slowly disengaging from Bosnia.

[33] Holbrooke, Richard, 1998, Op cit., p. 356.

[34] Holbrooke, Richard, 1998, Op cit., p. 352.

[35] See for a more detailed account, Bildt Carl, *Peace Journey*, 1998, chapter 10.

[36] When the OHR facilitated the Serb Ortodox Metropolit to celebrate mass in Sarajevo on the Orthodox Christmas day (January 8), RS television, operating from Pale, did not even run the story, as the possibility of coexistence did not fit the image that Pale TV was projecting night after night.

[37] Bildt, Op cit., p. 254.

[38] Chandler, David, *Bosnia, Faking Democracy after Dayton* (London: Pluto Press, 1998), p. 84.

[39] See list of appendices, No. 3.

[40] Westendorp, 1997a, in: Chandler, David, Op cit., pp. 111-112.

[41] Marchlewski, 1997, in: Chandler, David, Op cit., p. 137.

[42] The Citizens' Alternative Parliament is an association of Bosnian NGO's, which the OSCE saw as strengthening the work of NGO's. The OSCE's work with Displaced Person (DPs) groups was designed to feed in with the activities of the Coalition for Return, which is an association of refugee and displaced persons groups for Bosnia.

Chapter 5
A Critique of the Post-Dayton
Implementation Process

Introduction

The process of democratisation in BiH can be successful if it succeeds in creating a sense of representation and responsiveness, which forms the basis of *human security*. "Security is a policy discourse that has frequently worked to constitute political order rather than to initiate social change."[1] The aim of this chapter is to see how the post-Dayton implementation process initiates social change through the deconstruction of the established political order, namely the centralised nation state structure. As outlined in the previous chapter, there are many issues arising out of *the Accord* that are perceived as unjust. It is a prerequisite to *human security* that these issues by resolved, so as to instill a lasting peace.

Within this chapter the "burning issues" that hold the ability to create a lasting peace are critiqued and positively challenged. On a broader theoretical level these issues include the ability of the post-Dayton implementation process to foster more trusting and just relations between all ethnicities. The creation of a lasting peace depends largely upon the ability of the post-Dayton implementation process to implement *human security*. In this sense the success of post-Dayton implementation depends largely upon its ability to create a dispersal of sovereignty, with the aim of providing security for all peoples. Through the process of primary and secondary research accumulation[2] and aided by the theoretical underpinnings of this work, it became evident that there are a number of principal issues that must be positively challenged in the process of creating a lasting peace. Such issues, if positively challenged, hold the ability to help formulate a dispersed vertical and horizontal form of sovereignty. Within this chapter these "burning issues" are firstly outlined. Such "burning issues" relate to the process of refugee return, the significance of the electoral system, the function of humanitarian and developmental organisations and the role of political institutions.[3]

Thereafter on a theoretical level the significance of these "burning issues" is brought to bear, by the fact that success in such fundamental areas would allow for the continual development of dispersed forms of vertical and horizontal sovereignty.

Dayton's Failure to Create a State Represents its Success

As outlined in chapter three, the constellation of state centric ethno-nationalism in the Balkans was created as a result of the changing face of sovereignty. It is the aim here to analyse whether the developments in BiH since the signing of the *Dayton Peace Accord* have challenged state centric ethno-nationalism, insofar as Dayton implementation has resulted in new formulations of sovereignty. It is hugely important to note at this juncture that both the architects of *Dayton* and its implementers (principally the Office of the High Representative) were and are *not* attempting to create new sovereign formulations, but rather see as their task the eventual creation of a conventional sovereign Bosnia, based upon the Westphalia model. For this reason the *Dayton Peace Accord* and indeed its implementation is largely regarded as a failure. However, it is argued within this work that the failure to implement the Westphalian variant in Bosnia, and the novel, although still nascent, structures that have been created out of necessity, supposedly as stepping stones to the eventual creation of a Westphalian model, represent signposts as to how post-Westpahialian variants of social organisation may be created in the future. It is also significant to point out that the creation of the Westphalian model of nation state is not feasible in Bosnia, as it can only lead to fratricidal struggle between opposing identities. In summation, the implementation of Dayton is failing every day to create a sovereign unitary nation state. The structures created at *Dayton* and the implementation process reflects the socio-political topography of the region. For this reasons an analysis of post-Dayton implementation may signpost the means by which *human security* can be constructed in the future. Dayton implementation is by no means completely successful or indeed finished, put is does signpost how a world imploding with nationalism may de remade. What I propose, therefore, in this chapter is to analyse the extent to which developments within BiH mark a departure from the state-centric model. Such a departure is necessary, as "the state-centric prism offers no penetrating perspective on the dynamics of internal social contradictions or tensions, either within or beyond individual states".[4]

The Need for Electoral Reform

There are a number of significant issues which warrant research, insofar as they hold the ability to create space, represent identities and respond to issues of justice. *Electoral reform* is the first of those issues, insofar as electoral reform holds the ability to promote positive change in so many other politically sensitive areas. Currently, electoral break down clearly follows ethnic lines of division. In the sitting parliaments of BiH which were elected on November 11, 2000, for example, this reality is visible. In the Federation House of Representatives, the principal Serb nationalist party, the SDS, has no representation, while in the Republika Srpska National Assembly the HDZ, which is the principal Croat nationalist political party, received a vote of less than one percent. Meanwhile, the Serb national party, the SDS, holds 38% of the vote in the Republika Srpska national assembly, while in the Federation House of Representatives the two prominent Muslim parties, namely the SDA and SBIH, make up 42% of the vote.

If a more inclusive and multi-ethnic Bosnia is to be fashioned, multi-ethnic and inclusive political parties, such as the SDP must garner greater support. [5] Strongly nationalist parties serve to maintain monolithic national loyalty and promote spatial exclusion, based upon ethnicity. In this sense the SDS promote, through their actions and policies, an ethnically homogenous nation state of Republika Srpska, while the SDA promotes a Muslim Bosnia and the deconstruction of the entities created by Dayton. Less nationalist parties find it difficult to garner support, due to the level of ethnic insecurity, which is constantly re-articulated by the principal nationalist parties. However, the 2000 general election signalled the development of less natioanlist politics, at least among the Muslim population. For example, the moderate SDP (a multi-ethnic party, which is supported mainly by moderate Muslims) attained 5% of the vote in the RS national assembly, as compared to a 2% vote in the 1998 general election. In the vote for Federation House of Representatives, the SDP received 26% of the vote, as opposed to 14% in the 1998 elections.

The waning of ultra-nationalistic political parties is necessary in order to reach success in other sensitive areas such as refugee return, the return of displaced persons and education policy. However, the election manifested the continued strength of ethno-nationalism, with the Croat national party receiving 18% in the federation elections for the House of Representatives, down only 2% on the 1998 elections. Again the principal Serb nationalist party, the SDS, made considerably gains on the 1998 election.

The OSCE published a new election draft in 2000 with the aim of creating feasible avenues capable of delivering a greater sense of people representation. In such an environment, the nationalist parties would find it increasingly difficult to control power. On a more primal level, the strengthening of non-nationalist political parties would greatly reduce fear and insecurity amongst minority ethnicities. For example, from my field research I found that the few Bosnian Serbs still living in the Sarajevo suburb of Vogosca, which was a pre-war Bosnian Serb area, feel a great sense of alienation and insecurity, *not* because of the small size and stature of the political parties that represent them in predominantly Muslim Sarajevo, but rather because they feel that the dominant Muslim parties are anti-Bosnian Serb. The success of the SDP in the recent elections should, at least incrementally, help to resolve such fear. If fears and ethnic insecurities can be curtailed, voters will not feel the same need to vote for the most ultra-nationalist party on the electoral sheet of their ethnic persuasion.

The Return of Refugees and Displaced Persons

Return of Refugees and Displaced Persons (DPs) is fundamental to unlocking enduring peace in the region. The prioritisation and significance of this process shall be critiqued later in the chapter. "Since 1996 a total of 310,000 refugees returned to Bosnia and a further 250,000 displaced persons went home. But at the start of 1999, there were still 400,000 Bosnian refugees and 800,000 displaced persons waiting to restart their lives."[6] Although 1998 was declared the year of minority returns, only 100,000 refugees returned home. What is even more worrying and potentially more dangerous is the fact that very few returns took place in circumstances where the returnee would be returning to a region dominated by another ethnicity (so called minority returns). Humanitarian officials believe that the large majority of those still waiting to return fall into this category.[7] Nationalist parties pay lip service to the ideal of minority returns, but in reality they hinder the development of a multi-ethnic society at every juncture. The main tool utilised by the ultra nationalists in order to prevent returns is bureaucratic red tape.[8]

The question of minority return is fundamental to the development of peace in BiH, insofar as greater minority returns would allow the institutional framework created by Dayton to function in a more representative manner, thereby decoupling the modernity correlation between territory and nation, and subsequently institutionalising overlapping identity membership. As outlined in the previous chapter, the territorial settlement deriving from Dayton is felt to be unjust, nevertheless, given the forces that are at play there is no real possibility that the territorial settlement can be altered in any manner.[9] Institutionalising overlapping identity membership would have the effect of reducing the significance of the territorial question. However, the success of this process demands the return of refugees and displaced persons, so as to create multiple identity jurisdictions. For example, in the town of Brcko, I carried out informal interviews with Bosnian Serbs who migrated there from the Federation during and after the war. Most had a burning desire to return to their pre-war homes, however to do so would mean crossing the Inter Entity Boundary Line and thus succumbing to the stigma that entails life as an ethnic minority. However, if the return process could be accommodated and facilitated in the interest of the returning minorities, the process would help deliver a multi-ethnic BiH, as Serbs vacating Brcko and returning to the Federation, would simultaneously allow Muslims living in the Federation return to their pre-war homes in Brcko. Consequently this process would have the effect of destroying the relevance of the war created ethnic composition of BiH. Year 2000 certainly represented a watershed, with the return of minorities to their pre-war villages and towns, doubling the 1999 figures, which incidentally were considered high. In 2000 there were 67,000 minority returns in total. It is forecast that this process will continue unabated into 2001.

The Importance of Non-Governmental Organisations

In both promoting the return process and in encouraging the ethos of multi-ethnicity, *the Non Governmental Organisation sector* is one area warranting research, insofar as NGOs are necessary in order to form a horizontal dispersed sovereignty (see chapter two). In 1999 there were 136 international NGOs in BiH and 284 national NGOs.[10] In co-ordination with NGOs, organisations such as the United Nations Development Programme (UNDP) help finance and reconstruct society. Organisations such as the European Community Humanitarian Office (ECHO) work in partnership with NGOs, UN agencies and other international bodies such as the International Committee of the Red Cross. In the long term the creation of representative and decentralised political institutions should be able to create a durable and representative form of horizontal sovereignty. In the short term NGOs must be commended, in the case of Bosnia, for attempting to answer the immediate challenges. The co-ordination between NGOs and international humanitarian/developmental/political institutions and international donors must be welcomed, as it helps bring the people closer to power, be it economic, political or social.

The Significance of the Multi-Layered Political Structure

Institution Building and Political Structure are areas of great significance, as they represent the key to building an inclusive Bosnia. It is my task to analyse the extent to which the institutional structures allow the "creation of space". In this sense, I wish to critique particularly the "connective tissue" which links the common institutions (the Presidency, Council of Ministers) with the entities.[11] I also wish to critique the significance of municipalities and cantons, analysing the extent to which they instill horizontal sovereignty by responding to local need and specifications. Within the Federation, cantons, because of their restrictive territorial character, should possess the ability to respond and represent the unique ethnic make-up of a specific region. Added to that, the legislative power of the canton subtracts power, prestige and symbolism away from the state level and thus acts as a safeguard against the constellation of a state centrist approach. Within Republika Srpska (RS) common institutions should safeguard the interests of minority groups and should prevent RS becoming a centralised state. Common institutions *potentially* possess the ability to "decode" monolithic national identity and loyalty. In addition, municipalities within the RS hold a larger degree of power and influence than their counterparts in the Federation. Strong local government should prevent the RS assembly from becoming a ubiquitous force. In essence the fact that the RS is merely a constituent part of the Federation of BiH, in addition to the strength of local government should act as a safety network for minorities.[12]

The Case of Brcko

Finally, I wish to undertake a case study analysis of the special district of Brcko, which represents a rather unique example of dispersed vertical sovereignty. The autonomous Brcko district was created under the arbitration of the Brcko tribunal on March 5th 1999. The Brcko district comprises the entire territory of the pre-war Brcko municipality. The territory of the District is held by both entities, the Republika Srpska and the Federation, simultaneously. Allowing both entities to claim sovereignty over the district, whilst simultaneously "creating" the district as an autonomous region, is perhaps the most radical departure from the traditional notion of state sovereignty in contemporary International Relations. In relation to this work the question that must be posed is whether the deconstruction of orthodox sovereignty, in the Brcko region, and the reconstruction of a form of dispersed vertical and horizontal sovereignty creates the space necessary to include all identities and thereby enhance societal security.[13]

Minority Returns

"All refugees and displaced persons have the right freely to return to their homes of origin. They have the right, in accordance with Annex 7 of the General Framework Agreement, to have restored to them property of which they were deprived in the course of hostilities since 1991 and to be compensated for any such property that cannot be restored to them. Any commitments or statements relating to such property made under duress are null and void."[14] It is clear from the constitution that the return of refugees and displaced persons is stipulated and indeed has been vigorously encouraged by the Office of the High Representative. The process of return, although painstakingly slow, is making clear and certain progress. Within 1998 alone, which was dubbed "the year of returns" over 140,000 returns took place to and within BiH. There remain almost 31,000 refugees from BiH in Croatia, 210,000 BiH refugees in the Federal Republic of Yugoslavia, as well as some 130,000 refugees in Western Europe. At the end of 1998, the overall number of returnees to Bosnia and Herzegovina from abroad, inclusive of estimates of spontaneous returns, did not exceed 110,000. This figure is lower than the planning assumptions for 1998, which forecasted a range of 140,000 to 200,000 returns.

One of the factors which possibly slowed down the rate of refugee return, was the fact that most returnees were obliged to relocate to majority areas, mostly in the Federation, in the absence of conditions conducive to minority return to pre-war dwellings. There are some 860,000 internally displaced persons in BiH. What is most worrying is the fact that there are still such a high number of displaced persons within BiH who have not yet returned to their homes. Considering that six years have elapsed since the signing of the *Dayton Peace Accord*, there is a strong possibility that a certain percentage of internally displaced persons and indeed refugees have consciously decided to remain where they now reside. However, through my research I have found that there are nevertheless a large number who wish to return home. The major obstacle at this stage, however, is the fact that a great number of those who now want to return find themselves in the category of minority returns. There is a great insecurity and overt fear amongst many Muslims to return to their Serb nominated pre-war home in Republika Srpska, while many Serbs, for example, would fear alienation and socio-political exclusion if they were to return to their pre-war homes in Sarajevo.[15] This is the situation throughout the country and explains why only 35,000 to 40,000 of the 140,000 returns that occurred in 1998 were in fact minority returns.[16] Added to the slow progress regarding minority returns, there have also been a disappointingly small number of returns to Republika Srpska. Besides concerns about the security environment, people are also prevented from returning by inadequate material conditions, including the lack of available housing, employment, social services, as well as a low level of infrastructure and communications. Nevertheless there have been 125,000 minority returns since the signing of Dayton. However there are still about 1.6 million Bosnian refugees and displaced persons (DPs). Although as stated previously, the increase in minority returns in year 2000 manifests that the process may now finally be gaining momentum.

The Role and Success of the Reconstruction and Return Task Force

So as to facilitate a greater level of return, particularly minority returns and second phase returns[17] a comprehensive Reconstruction and Return Task Force (RRTF) network was established in February 1997 under the chairmanship of the OHR, and now exists on the ground. The RRTF operates across BiH. It has a counterpart in Croatia. The RRTF plan for 1999, set out an intensive programme to address the three issues of space (generating for people to return to), security (for individual returnees) and sustainability (making it possible for returnees to build a future in their home area), and included specific sector plans such as a substantial information campaign. As well as promoting returns from Western Europe, the RRTF urges the removal of all legislative and administrative obstacles to return, establishing and implementing property[18] and housing legislation, and other legislation necessary for progress in minority returns. The integrated approach of the RRTF is crucial, as these problems cannot be solved in a partial or isolated manner. The plan makes clear that the realisation of a long awaited for breakthrough in minority returns will require the international community to launch an all-out effort and focus all political leverage, economic resources and security assets, in order to create the basis for future self sustaining movements.[19] The success of the RRTF can be seen in the figures released for the January-March period of 1999, with minority returns of 1116, compared to 673 minority returns in the same period the previous year.[20] Privately the OHR estimated minority returns in the region of 120,000 for 1999,[21] however this figure was always going to be unreachable. A large increase in minority returns is nevertheless feasible in future years, and the momentum of spontaneous returns witnessed in 1999 did continue unabated throughout 2000.[22]

The Case of Mostar

In analysing the success of RRTF and indeed the degree to which refugees and displaced persons are returning, a case study critique of canton 7, which encompasses the city of Mostar serves as a litmus test, considering that the canton is both heavily Croat dominated and extremely nationalist. Added to that the city of Mostar itself represents a haven of sectarianism, physically divided into Croat and Muslim enclaves demarcated by the river. In the cantonal elections held in 2000, the Croat ethno-nationalist HDZ received 46% of the vote, this explains in itself why Muslim and Serb minorities may fear to return to their pre-war homes in Mostar. Successful minority returns in the region would not only serve to promote healing between peoples, but it would also allow the political institutions operate as they should, in this manner facilitating the generation of space and security. Although the situation is still quite tense in the region there has been an increase in returns into the Mostar area.[23] At the end of September 1999, UNHCR Sub-Office Mostar reported that over the summer months, some 250 ethnic Serbs had returned to areas in Herzegovina under both Bosnian Croat and Bosniak control. Moreover, 4,000 to 5,000 Bosnian Serbs had also indicated their desire to return to the Mostar region.

A new trend emerged, wherein a growing number of Bosnian Croats requested international assistance to return to minority areas, ignoring pressure by Bosnian Croat leaders who wished to discourage minority returns of Croats to other areas, so as to maintain a Croat monolithic identity in canton 7.[24] Meanwhile, Bosniak and Bosnian Serb minority returns are slowly continuing in canton 7, despite obstruction by the Bosnian Croat authorities on such issues as access to education, health care etc. Sub-Office Mostar also reported significant Bosniak and Bosnian Serb returns to Croat-administered areas in Slolac and Caplijna municipalities,[25] as well as in Mostar south, in September and October 1999. (At the time of writing, March 2001, the situation is very sense in Mostar as the Croat nationalist political party, the HDZ, are attempting to establish an illegal entity assembly in the city.)

The Return Process in Republika Srpska

Again, the process of return in Republika Srpska is obstructed and much slower than wished; however, certain success is being achieved. For example, in 1996, after the signing of the *Dayton Peace Accord*, there were no refugee minority returns to RS, whilst 7,925 Serbs (the dominant ethnicity in RS) moved into the region. In 1998, however, 1,279 Bosniaks and 257 Bosnian Croat refugees returned, as minorities, to RS.[26] If we look at the situation regarding internally displaced persons, one finds a similar trend. Whereas a mere 136 Bosniak DP's returned to RS in 1996, 6,765 Bosniak DP's returned in 1998. The statistics manifest two significant factors; firstly, the process of return is a slow and arduous task. Secondly, it would appear time is an important variable, in allowing confidence and trust develop, which invariably facilitates minority returns. It would appear thus that minority returns are likely to increase rather then decrease with time. The identical process appears to be occurring in the Federation. In 1996, for example, only 1,179 Serb DP's returned to the Federation, where they are an ethnic minority. Whilst in 1998, 6,058 Serb DP's returned to the Federation. One of the more successful mechanisms developed so as to accelerate the pace of return has been the establishment of the Office of the Human Rights Ombudsman for BiH. The office has been instrumental in promoting property law and attempting to transform the principles of the European Convention on Human Rights into reality in BiH. Specifically regarding the issue of Refugees and DP's in Bosnia, the Ombudsman attempts to work with the local authorities so as to facilitate returns, often issuing recommendations and suggestions regarding specific cases, or perhaps institutes proceedings before the Human Rights chamber.

Means of Building Trust

One method introduced by the Organisation for Security and Cooperation in Europe (OSCE) so as to increase trust and security amongst possible future minority returnees, has been to implement a programme that concentrates on returning minority elected officials to their pre-war constituency. It is felt that if minorities have elected representation permanently stationed and living in their original home constituency, their constituents will find it easier to return home, knowing that they are politically represented. "In reality it is a confidence building measure, as it is a lack of confidence in the system that is preventing a greater number of returns."[27] In the Banja Luka region for example, there were 317 displaced elected   officials   after   the   1997   municipal   elections.   Through encouragement from the OSCE and facilitation by RRTF/NGO's a total of 28 elected officials had returned to their homes by the end of May 1999. In Bugojno, a municipality in the region of Banja Luka, there were 7 displaced elected officials affiliated to the Croat HDZ political party. By May 1st 1999, one of these councilors had returned, while one had been given keys to accommodation without yet returning. Meanwhile the RRTF in coordination with NGO's prepared 3 houses in the area for elected officials. This project is becoming more successful according to the Priority Return Officer with the OSCE in Banja Luka, she points to the fact that all 26 displaced officials in Prijedor had been granted access to return by the municipality, although they had not as of yet returned (August 1999). The significance of the process of return is paramount to the sustaining of peace in BiH, as shall be outlined in greater theoretical depth in the next chapter The above account documents progress in relation to the return process and although the process is painstakingly difficult, it is obvious that the adaptation of specific mechanisms (RRTF, Human Rights Ombudsman[28]) and the passing of time is aiding the acceleration of the process.

Reconciliation Through Electoral Reform

The concept of separate ethnic identities is deeply rooted in Bosnian society. These identities were formed during more than four centuries of Ottoman rule and reflect the unique structure of that empire's administration, namely the *millet* system, which allowed all religious communities, Muslim, Orthodox and Catholic, to effectively govern themselves. These separate identities have remained clearly defined in the 20th century, being institutionalised in the constitutions of the former Yugoslavia. Again the *Dayton Peace Accord* appears to institutionalise this structure, which is not surprising considering that the agreement was constructed between the ethnically based parties that waged war against each other for three years and nine months. It is hardly surprising therefore that the constitution contains a series of provisions which appear designed to ensure that those same parties remain entrenched in power indefinitely. For example, at the Presidential level, the Agreement states, "the Presidency of Bosnia and Herzegovina shall consist of three Members: one Bosniak and one Croat, *each directly elected from the territory of the Federation,* and one Serb *directly elected from the territory of the Republika Srpska.*[29] This provision which prevents Serbs and Others[30] running for presidential election in the Federation and Croats, Bosniaks and Others from running in Republika Srpska makes it considerably more difficult to construct an electoral system designed to promote moderation and reconciliation."[31]

As outlined earlier in this chapter, ethno-nationalist parties wield political power in the Balkans today. The Croat HDZ, Serb SDS and Bosniak SDA are strongly ethnic-based parties, having controlled the political landscape in BiH since the first elections after the war in 1996.[32] Such political parties are characterised by an "anti-integration" ethos. For example, the HDZ affiliated Mayors of Mostar, Capljina, Stolac and Ravno refused to attend a regional meeting of Mayors (4 November 1999) from both Eastern Herzegoovina (RS) and Herzegovina-Neretva Canton (Federation). The meeting which was held in order to discuss the issue of refugees and DPs, was marked by the absence of the above Mayors and points to the difficulty in promoting reconciliation as long as ethno-nationalist politicians control the rains of power.[33] As a form of response to anti-integration elements, the OSCE formulated a new election law draft (July 1999) aiming to foster more moderate politics, reconciliation and accountability.[34] Such progress is certainly required as ethno-nationalist parties have been to the fore in hindering and bureaucratically obstructing the return of refugees and displaced persons. Added to that, the working of the institutional structures created under the DPA has been hampered consistently by ethno-nationalist political parties. The current situation in canton 7 manifests the magnitude of this problem. Croats and Muslims refuse to meet in a common assembly in canton 7, for example, making the drafting of legislation almost impossible. Moreover, the nationalist political parties in canton 7 excessively utilise the veto provision written into the DPA to protect the vital interest of an ethnic community.[35]

The Significance of New Election Legislation

There are a number of provisions within the new election draft that were aimed to promote reconciliatory politics. Firstly a preferential vote system for the members of the Presidency of BiH and the President and the Vice-President of the RS, was incorporated into the draft Permanent Election Law. This allows voters to rank candidates in order of preference. In order to attract these preferences, candidates invariably must move away from extremist positions and appeal to inter ethnic interests. Up until this point citizens simply voted for one candidate, invariably of their ethnicity. Not only did this allow extreme nationalists to get elected (such as former President of the RS national assembly, Mr. Poplasen, who was displaced last spring 1999 by the OHR for generally obstructing reconciliation) but also the structure caused minority ethnicity's to feel alienated from the process. One can see this in the 1998 presidential election where 17.19% of votes for the Serb member of the BiH presidency were invalid. Practically all of those 17.19% invalid votes were unmarked ballots indicating a conscious decision by *certain* voters *not* to select any of the eligible candidates. In this case it would appear that Bosniak and Croat voters living in RS did not support any of the candidates running for presidency, as all candidates were Serbian. However, in a preferential system those prior disillusioned voters will have the power to influence the outcome of the election in some sense, insofar as they can give first preference to the least nationalist candidate and thereby promote the chances of such a candidate being elected. In the previous system, where voters choose only one candidate there was never the slightest possibility that dissident voters could influence the outcome in any way.

To Bring Moderate Politics to the Fore   Along with the preferential voting system the new election law draft attempts to ensure that presidential candidates running for election are somewhat moderate in character, insofar as they must obtain a certain percentage of signatures of support from voters who hold permanent residence and still live in a different entity or obtain the support of a municipal in a different entity. This should encourage more moderate policies, as parties are required to garner support cross-entity in the pre-election period. In addition, for all bodies of authority at all levels, parties and coalitions shall put forward open candidate lists so that voters are able to express their preference not only for a party or coalition but also for the candidates whom they support. It was hoped that this would allow voters to express their preference for particular candidates. The open list system should reduce the intensity of ethnic voting, insofar as citizens now have the choice of evaluating a candidate, rather than simply voting for the party that represents their ethnicity. This is borne out in a poll carried out in June 1999 by the OSCE where 67 percent of those polled said they would pay the most attention to the character and capabilities of the candidate, while only 21 percent said they would pay the most attention to the nationality or ethnicity of the candidate.[36]   Once the voters directly elect candidates, elected representatives will also have to become responsive to the electorate if they are to be re-elected.

Following the municipal election that took place in April 2000 minor changes were made to the draft election law resulting from the experiences of managing the municipal election. Principally, the law remains the same, except the draft offers one new option, requiring candidates for the BiH Presidency to run on a joint ticket made up of candidates from all three constituent peoples. Such a measure would have the beneficial effect of creating a Presidency with a pre-arranged program of *cooperation*. This law will come into effect for the 2002 presidential election.

In October 2000, one month before the general elections, another modification to the election law was introduced. This modification was to apply to the November 2000 general election and again was introduced so as to bring moderate politics to the fore. The new rule was intended to give smaller parties in the Cantonal assemblies a voice in the selection of the Federation House of Peoples. It would make potential representatives to the House eof Peoples more moderate and representative, as they would be elected by popular vote to the House of Peoples, rather than selected by their parties, which was the basis of the old system. Of course in order to be elected by popular vote, candidates would greatly increase their chances if they could appeal to more than one ethnicity. This new modification to the election rules is without doubt a good ruling, as it should help the fostering of human security in bringing moderate politics to the fore. However, it was a mistake to introduce the modification just one month before the national elections, as it made nationalist parties, who were already involved in a heated election campaign, feel that the International Community was attempting to suppress them. The HDZ were particularly infuriated by the ruling, as they realised that their sectarian politics would win them no friends outside their own party in a popular cantonal vote for House of Peoples representation. The decision of the HDZ to illegally establish a third entity in Mostar in March 2001 was certainly catalysed by this new electoral modification.

Stipulated Female Political Participation   A most interesting facet of the new electoral draft is the fact that female political participation has been acknowledged by the law's drafters as critical to BiH's successful transition to democracy. The draft law incorporates a provision that mandates that at least one-third of the candidates on the candidates' list must be women and that they must be equally distributed throughout the list. The new electoral stipulation, by urging women into the traditional "public" patriarchal arena, not only promotes the empowerment of women, but also should lead to greater inter-ethnic co-operation, as women tend to put a greater emphasis upon *human security* and co-operation than men.[37] The OSCE has continued to support the entry of women into the public arena. In fact in November and December of 1999, the OSCE, with assistance from the Norwegian government, organised a cross-country series of seminars ("Women can do it seminars") aimed at helping women increase their presence on the political scene in BiH. The overall goals of the "Women can do it" programme included encouraging women to play a proactive role in politics and public life, fostering nation-wide grassroots movements, and enabling women from different political parties, NGOs and trade unions to develop their political skills. As stated by Robert Barry, the OSCE Head of Mission in BiH, "more women in local politics mean a democratic process that is more tolerant".[38]

Finally the electoral reforms still preserve the right of refugees and displaced persons to vote in the municipalities of their pre-war homes and also preserve "Out of Country Voting".[39] It is very important that these rights be preserved as the ability to vote in one's pre-war constituency helps create multi-ethnic constituencies, insofar as it is not only the people living in the region that have the right to vote, but also pre-war ethnicities are given a voice. Moreover, if the pre-war residents feel politically represented in their pre-war homes there obviously is a greater likelihood that they should feel secure enough to return.

The 2000 Municipal and National Elections

The failure of the BiH parliament to find the consensus necessary to ratify the draft election law is a certain set back in the creation of a pluralist and inclusive Bosnian society. Because of the failure to implement the draft, the Provisional Election Commission (PEC)[40] decided to impose the draft for the general elections to be held in Autumn 2000, with the aim of instilling the democratisation process. The PEC already initiated this process in relation to the April 2000 municipal elections to great effect.[41] Regarding the municipal elections, the PEC in line with the draft election law, implemented an open candidate list system, redrafted property legislation which prevented illegal occupants from running in the municipal elections, stipulated female political participation and finally preserved the right of refugees and displaced persons to vote in the municipalities of their pre-war homes.[42]

The provisions implemented by the PEC had a significantly positive effect upon the municipal elections in helping to create a pluralist society. "Nationalism may not be on the run yet-witness the strength of indicated Bosnian Serb war criminal Radovan Karadzic's Serbian Democratic Party (SDS), but moderate leaders are making inroads and increasing numbers of voters seem to be paying attention to their messages."[43] For example, women now fill 18 per cent of the seats in BiH's elected municipal legislatures, creating a more gender representative parliament. In addition both the SBiH and the SDP, two moderate Bosniak parties polled well and thus curtailed the influence of the ethno-nationalist SDA Bosniak party. In RS, while the nationalist SDS polled well, it must be remembered that many would be SRS voters voted instead for the SDS, as the extreme nationalist SRS were banned from running in the election by the OHR for failing to promote peace and reconciliation. Most significantly in RS, Mladen Ivanic's moderate Party of Democratic Progress (PDP) were successful and the moderate Ivanic was earmarked after the election as a possible future RS Prime Minister. In Herzog-Bosna the low turnout strongly signified the waning of support for the ethno-national HDZ. The rise of genuine democratic, non-nationalist alternatives among both the Bosniaks and Serbs, as seen in polling results for the SDP, SNSD, and the PDP, and the dramatic fall in voter turnout in the more radical HDZ controlled regions, should allow the municipal political system in BiH operate in a more integrative and cooperative fashion. It was hoped that if similar results to the municipal elections were repeated in the General Election in Autumn 2000, sensitive issues such as dismantling of the three ethnic armies (which Dayton allowed exist)[44] could be tackled in a fundamental manner.

The results of the general elections were not, however, so positive as the municipal elections. Both the HDZ and SDA secured a strong result in the federation, manifesting that ethno-nationalism is still healthy in Bosnia. Nevertheless both parties have been kept out of government in the Federation House of Representatives. The new government came into existence on March 12, 2001 and consists of a 10 party coalition, referred to as the Alliance for Change. The two principal parties of this coalition are the SDP, a moderate multi-ethnic party and the SBIH, a Muslim party with a progressive relatively moderate stance. Interestingly, the SBIH, which is a break-away party from the SDA, stated that it would not go into coalition with the corrupt, Muslim nationalist SDA party.

In the RS the strong showing of the SDS again manifests the continued influence of nationalist parties However they were unable to form a single government and have formed a coalition with the more moderate PDP. The leader of the PDP, Mladan Ivanic has also become Prime Minister and has promised to work towards reform and integarion.

Perhaps the greatest achievement has been the formation of a Council of Ministers (the executive of Bosnia and Herzegovina) which does not include any of the parties that have ruled the country for the last ten years. This is the first time sense 1990, that a somewhat moderate Council of Ministers has been formed. It is hoped now that the Council of Ministers can become the engine room of change and progress. If it does it will allow the Office of the High Representative to take a lesser role in directing governance. A successful Council of Ministers could also tackle economic reform, which of course is the key to destroying ethno-sectarianism. The new Chairman of the Council of Ministers, Dr. Bozidar Matic is a member of the SDP, a party that supports a multi-ethnic ethos. He has pledged his support to overcoming nationalism and promoting economic development. In the Federation 10 party coalition government, the Alliance for Change have elected a Croat as President, Mr. Karlo Filpovic, he is also a member of the SDP and along with the Federation Prime Minister Alija Behmen, promoted an extensible progressive government program. In RS, the influence of the PDP and Prime Minister Ivanic upon the SDS, together with both the growing influence of the SDP and the watchful eye of the OHR, should maintain a working entity.

The most fundamental obstacle facing Bosnia today is the obstructionist tactics deployed by the HDZ, which culminated in the forming if an illegal parliament in Mostar in March of 2001. As stated previously my primary research has shown that a working peace in Bosnia requires progress in four fundamental areas. One of those areas relates to effective political institutions. The actions of the HDZ are dictatorial and undemocratic, largely representative of fear but not of people. If the party is unwilling to exercise its mandate and represent its people in a democratic sense, then the party has failed its people. It is important, however, that the Office of the High Representative does not ban the party, as suggested by many political commentators. To do so, would only exacerbate the sense of alienation obviously felt. Rather the HDZ need to be assured that Croat identity will neither be exterminated nor assimilated. A number of measures are presented in the next chapter as to how this may be achieved.

Humanitarian and Developmental Issues

There are two principal intertwined avenues by which a multi-ethnic, representative and responsive Bosnia can be created. Firstly the institutional structure created under the DPA, may deliver a vertical dispersal of sovereignty if progress is made on refugee return, political institution building and election reform. However, the ability of functional institutions to instill horizontal sovereignty, by responding to human need, is a precondition, as functional bodies help to destroy ethno-nationalism by breaking away from the traditional link between sovereignty and a definite territory. Such bodies, according to Mitrany, both set about developing policy according to social needs and in keeping with the needs of the give time. It is necessary that dispersed horizontal sovereignty is institutionalised and coordinated so as to deliver *human security*. This approach, based upon a broad functional ethos, can only succeed if national loyalties are decoded, as the effective development of functional institutions is undermined by the existence of monolithic nationalist loyalties. As explained in chapter two, in countering ethno-nationalism, which prevents the adoption of *human security*, a redefinition of space and a celebration of multiple identity membership is a prerequisite. To this end the proper functioning of vertical structures will in time facilitate the emancipation of identities, while horizontal structures, namely municipalities' and non-governmental functional organisations, play a larger role in delivering such emancipation in a tangible manner.

At this stage, six years after the signing of the *Dayton Peace Accord*, the role of non-state actors, NGOs and community organisations is paramount in helping create a sense of solidarity, as the institutions on the vertical axis have not yet wholly delivered emancipation for all identities at a political level. NGOs are particularly necessary in order to challenge the benign neglect suffered by large sections of all communities. Secondly, they undoubtedly help bring local people into the process of governance, thus building the capacity and educating local peoples into the process of democratisation.[45]

The proper functioning of horizontal sovereignty will undoubtedly have a positive effect upon the vertical axis, creating a more educated, less nationalist electorate. In addition, educating the people into the process of democratisation is fundamental if the needs and challenges of local peoples are to be met. The Independent Bureau for Humanitarian Issues (IBHI), one such national NGO, which aims to build local capacity, helps in the implementation programme re: DPA, and encourages training of municipality officials. It believes that "international and other organisations operating within the sphere of social reconstruction must recognise that it is neither desirable nor appropriate that they should act or be perceived to replace the governmental authority in BiH. The policy and practice of these organisation must be guided by an ethos of 'unsung assistance', strengthening local human, institutional and governmental capacities...."[46]

Since the signing of the GFAP, non-state actors, NGOs and community organisations have had mammoth success in tackling social issues. Nevertheless social marginalisation is still alarmingly high. At the end of 1998, 58% of the population in BiH had been in a state of poverty. Even those in employment suffer a degree of impoverishment; in fact 25% of those who are employed earn salaries that only cover up to 65% of the cost of their "consumer basket" of basic needs.[47] Vulnerable groups such as the disabled and the old also suffer. In fact pensioners are faced with serious difficulties because pensions in BiH are usually paid after a delay of two months. About 60% of BiH's population require some form of social protection in order to live normally. Currently such social protection does not formally exist, but is instead provided through informal means. "The high level of solidarity among relatives, financial help from relatives and friends abroad, international humanitarian organisations' support for a considerable number of 'vulnerable' groups (mostly the elderly, handicapped, returnees and the ill) and the municipalities, through the system of exceptional social assistance, are addressing the most threatened cases."[48] Since 1996 these informal means of social protection are becoming more co-ordinated, structured and institutionalised and at this stage even the local organs of power have influence regarding distribution.

The ethos of "development from below" established firstly by NGOs has gained credence within the institutional structure of BiH. Not only does such an ethos prove to be more flexible and efficient, but it also helps to empower local people, thus transforming the dependency culture that has existed in BiH since 1995 (and before). The involvement of local developmental organisations, run by local people, plus the International Community's support for municipalities and local enterprises, is helping to create a culture of self-help. Such an ethos both helps construct human solidarity and secondly alleviates the Kantian all-purpose image of the state, as traditional state functions are now beginning to be executed at the local level.

The Political Structure in BiH

The dis-aggregation of authority away from the state centric model is the most fundamental aspect of the political structure of the national government of BiH.[49] This structure potentially may create a sense of overlapping identities and multiple spatialities. However, as stated previously the burning issues outlined earlier in this chapter must be fundamentally tackled if this is to be the case. Within the Federation, power is directed towards the local.[50] As stated by Peter Krale (European Community Monitoring Mission to BiH) "the structure is highly decentralised, insofar as cantons control taxes and municipalities can use taxes as they will".[51] The Federation consists of ten cantons, whilst a municipal government controls each local region.[52] The citizens of that delineated region directly elect both cantonal and municipal assemblies. In this manner, municipal assemblies represent the ethnic make-up of the municipality, while the cantonal assembly again represents the specific fibre of a given larger delineated territory. The obvious benefit in having the institutions of power placed in such close proximity to the people is that it creates a greater sense of representation.

Obviously there may, nevertheless, be minorities within given cantons who feel alienated from the political structure. For example, in canton seven, Serbs and Muslims may feel alienated because of the strong position of Croats.[53] However, alienated Muslims will find themselves well represented within the Federation House of Representatives, while Serbs with poor representation at contonal level, will find representation at Council of Ministers level and within the BiH House of Peoples. Also those with minority representation at cantonal level may be quite well represented at municipal level where they hold numerical weight (Serbs in Bihac municipalities for example).[54]

The Joint Institutions – Aiming to Represent all Ethnicities

Ultimately of course those who feel alienated from the institutions at local level are certain of representation, although of a less tangible nature, at state level. The common institutions, therefore, comprising the tripartite presidency, the executive branch, the legislative branch and the judiciary, represent all groups.[55] The lack of co-operation and thus effectiveness within the common institutions, however, has hampered the growth of trust between entities. Morris Power, of the Refugee Return Task Force (RRTF), maintains that the common institutions have had extremely limited success since their creation in 1996 and that it is really only quite recently that they have begun to work together in areas of common concern such as the fight against crime.[56] Such areas of common concern have a functional character, as such issues transcend ethnic, physical and mental borders. Society as a whole is seen to benefit if crime can be curtailed.

The slow, but significant, progress in this regard can be seen with the establishment of a State Border Service (SBS), which will be directed at state level, by the Ministry of Civil Affairs and Communications. The SBS will have responsibility over border surveillance with the aim of reducing crime and shall be operated by police from both entities. At the New York Declaration (15 November 1999) the Presidents agreed that the SBS legislation would be submitted to the BiH parliament by November 24, 1999, and that the first units would be deployed by December 31, 1999. The Troika Presidency also declared in the New York Declaration that a permanent Secretariat for the joint Presidency shall be created, and that full funding of the state ministries is an essential prerequisite for a truly functioning state government. Both of these endeavours help solidify the joint institutions, thus creating stronger connective tissue between entities.

Political Representation within Republika Srpska

Within Republika Srpska the citizens also have the opportunity to directly elect delegates to the RS municipal assembly. Again as in the Federation the proximity of the institutions to the citizens should fairly reflect the ethnic make-up of specific regions. "Out of Country Voting" and the ability to vote in pre-war municipalities, means that Bosniak and Croats are at least partially represented at the municipal level in RS. As noted in the previous chapter, unlike the Federation there is no cantonal structure in RS, which invariably leaves the national parliament in a stronger position of influence than its counterpart in the Federation. However, as a slight counterweight to this, the municipal assemblies in RS also have greater influence and autonomy than their counterparts in the Federation. Nevertheless, many Muslims fear that Bosnian Serbs might attempt to attain nation state status for RS, by strengthening the Inter Entity Boundary Line and controlling the RS "national" parliament. In an interview Mr. Dzemal Subasic, senior advisor to the federation Minister for Social Policy, Displaced Persons and Refugees,[57] maintained that it is only when the canton system is also applied to RS will a multi-ethnic pluralist state be truly possible. It is certainly the case that the creation of a cantonal system in RS would be a progressive step towards creating a more representative governmental structure. However, due to the persisting strength of nationalist political parties in RS, there is little evidence that such a step will be taken at least in the short term.

Through primary research undertaken in RS, however, I found that the fears of Bosnian Muslims are largely unfounded, as the great majority of peoples living in RS see themselves as integral to the state of BiH, although being part of the nation of RS. For example, in manifesting this point, the IEBL is neither marked nor noticed as one crosses from RS to the Federation. In fact, most Bosnian Serbs today view it as a psychological border, rather than as a real border. If we contrast this situation with that of 1996 when Carl Bildt was unable to get the troika Presidency to meet in order to establish the common institutions, the essence of reconciliation is evident. Then the Bosnian Serb president, Krajisnik, refused to meet on the Federation side of the IEBL, while the Muslim president Izetbegovic refused to meet on the RS side of the IEBL. Eventually a compromise was found; a venue overlooking Sarajevo (federation), minutes away from the IEBL on the road to Pale (RS). Now, some five years later, there is constant traffic over the IEBL without any sense of conflict. In fact given that the peoples of Bosnia are socially and linguistically similar and given that there have been common licence plates in Bosnia since 1997, it would be impossible to differentiate a Serb from a non-Serb crossing the IEBL.

Within the RS national parliament there are 83 members directly elected. Because of the increase in minority returns, aided by the ability to vote in pre-war homes, Bosniak parties are growing in power within the RS parliament and up until the recent national elections they supported the moderate minority government.[58] In supporting the minority government, the SLOGA coalition,[59] the Bosniak and Croat parties received tangible support from the government and simultaneously kept the highly nationalist SDS/SRS parties out of government. Pasi Poysari, senior political adviser with the OHR in Banja Luka remarked to me in an interview that the political configuration in the previous RS national assembly manifested the ability and success of democracy. This indeed was the case, as the less nationalist SLOGA coalition was able to keep the extreme nationalist SDS out of power, ironically with the passive support of the Muslim SDA coalition. In the November 2000 national elections, the SDS reasserted its control on the RS parliament. However, it is interesting to note that the return of the SDS to government was dependent upon the support of a moderate Serb party, the PDP and particularly its leader Ivanic, who has become Prime Minister. The PDP, as a new political force in RS politics signifies that Serbs in RS, who make up the great majority of the population, are moving slowly towards a more moderate politics. It is true that the nationalist SDS increased its vote, but this increase was due to votes received from SRS voters, as the SRS was banned by the OHR before the election, because of their intense Serb nationalistic stance and obstruction to Dayton.

Although many Muslims fear that RS may slowly develop as an independent nation state, this is by no means the case and in fact RS is very much a constituent and integral part of BiH. For example, one only need account the commitment that BiH has made to supply the UN with a BiH police force for UN missions. This police force is made up of Federation and RS police and will serve under the common flag of BiH. This is a most symbolic point, as the police forces in BiH are controlled at entity level, thus the Federation and RS have separate police forces with different rules, regulations and uniforms. Nevertheless both police forces will melt into one for the purpose of UN participation, wearing different uniforms, but wearing the common BiH flag on the shoulder of their uniform.

The Role of the Office of the High Representative: A Push or a Shove?

The political structures created under the DPA are clearly ontopological[60] in nature, insofar as the institutions are obsessed with ethnic balance and ethnic representation, as a result of ethnic warfare. At the initial stage such ethnic balancing is necessary so as to safeguard the peoples of Bosnia who undoubtedly witnessed grotesque fratricidal barbarism for almost four years. There is evidence of co-operation, however, at all institutional levels that should in time help resolve ethnic tensions. The degree to which such co-operation is based upon common will or an external "shove" is an issue of great debate. It is a fact that the Office of the High Representative (OHR) plays a significant role in *promoting* co-operation between the political institutions.[61] Promoting such co-operation ironically often involves implementing binding decisions when/if the domestic institutional structures fail to find common ground. The failure of the BiH parliament, for example, to ratify the draft election law has meant that the PEC, an institution created by the OHR, has decided to implement the draft election law itself with provisions.

If one looks at some of the more controversial decisions taken by retired High Representative Westendorp, one attains a sense of the importance and influence of the OHR. For example the OHR issued common licence plates in BiH, because of the failure of the common institutions to make progress in this matter. Again the OHR issued common passports so as to increase the level of free movement within the country.[62] In March of 1999 High Representative Westendorp, displaced Mr. Poplasen, the President of Republika Srpska, because of Poplasen's intense degree of obstructionism. Again Zivko Radisic, Serb member of the tripartite presidency, was suspended by the High Representative for writing to the Hague Tribunal, withdrawing the charges pressed by BiH against the Federal Republic of Yugoslavia. On November 29, 1999 the OHR in conjunction with the OSCE decided to remove 22 elected officials from office for consistently pursuing anti-Dayton, anti-peace, anti-reconciliation and extra-legal agendas. Most recently the setting High Representative, Wolfgang Petritsch, removed Mr. Jelavic, the Croat member of the tripartite Presidency from office (March 7, 2001), because Jelavic ordered his HDZ party to establish an illegal parliament in Mostar in a bid to create a third entity. It remains to be seen whether the actions of the High Representative are successful in forcing the HDZ to return to the joint institutions.

The Fruitfulness of OHR Intervention

While it can be argued that such intervention by the international community is anti-democratic, it must be firstly kept in mind that the troika presidency supported many of the actions of the OHR.[63] Secondly, it is hoped by the OHR that such intervention should allow for the development of a more inclusive and co-operative politics. Thirdly, the Council of Ministers, as executive body, at least up until now have proven to be less the productive (the recently appointed Council of Ministers show much more promise), as national sectarianism has dogged any would be progress. For this reason the OHR was left with very little choice, but to act in its place.

The OHR intervention has proven successful on many accounts. From the interviews I conducted most interviewees from all ethnic backgrounds, pointed to the fact that common passports and common licence plates have promoted free movement, making the Inter Entity Boundary Line, no more than a psychological barrier. Again, the displacement of Mr. Poplasen gave former Prime Minister Dodic more leverage and influence in promoting more inclusive politics in RS. The OHR also in co-ordination with aid and developmental organisations has promoted reconciliation by less obvious means. For example, it used donor money as a weapon so as to promote progress on minority returns, inter-entity co-operation, and disarmament.

Apart from the pressure accrued through the international community, the institutional structures have also developed a momentum of their own, which has brought certain and tangible progress. The tripartite presidency, for example, has in general spoken in unison and in a constructive manner.[64] Co-operation between the entities is also improving. For example, recently progress has been made on military matters with the establishment of a standing committee at presidency level. Indeed progress in this field is vital as one of the great failings of the GFAP, was the fact that it allowed the existence of three armies within BiH. James Fergusson, public affairs spokesman for the OHR referred to this as a complete waste of money in an interview I conducted with him in August 1999. As noted by Fergusson, 40% of the federation budget is spent on military matters, while 18% of the RS budget is spent on maintaining the military. Would it not be better if this money were spent on social issues? This view is endorsed by the Standing Committee on Military Matters (SCMM), which was established by the OHR to promote the demilitarisation of the three ethnic armies.[65]

There has also been an improvement in cooperation at ministry level; particularly the ministries of the interior have been co-operating effectively. The effective establishment of the exhumation commission is probably one of the most successful joint entity endeavours.[66] The successful endeavour of the common institutions in this regard, considering the sensitivity and complexity of this process, shows the ability and extent to which the political institutions within BiH have matured since their establishment. Fergusson maintains that the growing trust and developing co-operation between the Federation and the RS is caused principally by the fact that RS under the leadership of Prime Minister Dodik began to look in the direction of Sarajevo rather than Belgrade (Recently elected RS Prime Minister Ivanic neither appears hostile to Sarajevo.) This argument is legitimised by the fact that the sacking of radical nationalist Serb Nikola Poplasen, the NATO bombing of Serbia and the final Brcko decision (which took Brcko out of the control of RS) failed to provoke the citizens of RS into protest or obstructionism. [67]

At municipal and cantonal level the reconciliation process appears to be totally based upon the personalities involved, the specific politicians. It can, therefore, be assumed that the development of the permanent election law, which promotes a more moderate politics, should influence all cantons and municipalities in a positive fashion. Apart from the issue of political personalities, the biggest obstacle preventing greater effectiveness at cantonal and municipal level throughout BiH, is both the citizen's lack of political education and understanding of the process of democratisation. To this end, the OSCE and ECHO along with certain national/international NGOs (eg. the National Democratic Institute) are attempting to educate citizens. However, this process will take time.

The fundamental question remains, however, can the developments within post-Dayton Bosnia lead to the adoption of workable dispersed vertical and horizontal sovereignty and ultimately result in greater *human security*? It is argued within this chapter that electoral reform, the NGO sector, the character of political parties/institutions and refugee return will all dialectically have an effect upon such a process. Within the next chapter, I critique the extent to which this process has occurred to date.

Notes

[1] Campbell, David, in: Dalby, 1994, Op cit., p. 2.
[2] I spent a ten-week period in Bosnia and Herzegovina in the summer of 1999, where I conducted fifty semi-structured interviews with relevant bodies in the cities of Sarajevo, Mostar, Banje Luka, and Brcko. By way of my primary research I located four primary areas

or issues which are vital to the development of inclusion and human security in BiH. I term such areas of concern as "burning issues", insofar as they each hold the ability to create space, by enabling the adoption of dispersed vertical and horizontal forms of sovereignty.

[3] There are several other areas of concern in post-Dayton Bosnia, including the stature of political economy, the political weight of the diasporas, the existence of mafias and the state of ecology. However, if the four fundamental "burning issues" critiqued within this chapter are challenged in a positive sense, all other areas of concern can only thereafter be positively challenged.

[4] Youngs, Gillian, *International Relations in a Global Age* (Cambridge: Polity Press, 1999), p. 40.

[5] Alexander Nitzsche (OSCE press officer, Sarajevo) reiterated to me by phone interview on May 15th 2000 that Social Democratic Party (SDP) victories in the municipal elections (April 8th 2000) signalled a long awaited and welcome change in the way the Bosnian electorate thinks and votes. In Bosniak majority areas they won relative or absolute majorities in 15 municipalities.

[6] Wilkinson, Ray (1999), "A Decisive Year", *Refugees*, Vol. 1, No. 114, p. 8.

[7] By July 1999, only 6,000 refugees had returned to Republika Srpska, which is a predominantly Serb entity. This slow rate of return is more clearly understood when we consider that 18,000 Bosniaks alone lived in Banja Luka (the capital of Republika Srpska) before the war. It would appear thus that Bosniaks fear to return to their pre-war home because they ethnically would be in minority. This information was obtained by interview (July 1999) with Mr. Dzemal Subasic, Senior advisor to Minister for Social policy, Displaced Persons and Refugees. See list of appendices, No. 1.

[8] There are 13 different constitutions and 13 different legal systems in BiH which allows nationalist parties to engage in bureaucratic warfare.

[9] To make an alteration to the territorial settlement stipulated at Dayton, would require Croatian Serbian and Bosnian representatives to agree a new territorial configuration which is beyond the realms of possibility given the complexity of the issue.

[10] Currently there are 242 organisation involved in Education/Training, 205 dealing with children youth; 194 involved with human rights; 190 dealing with returns; 178 dealing with civil society; 169 dealing with humanitarian, 156 involved with women; 154 dealing with psycho-social issues; 133 dealing with information/media; 129 dealing with health issues; 122 involved with micro-credit/income generation; 122 dealing with shelter/reconstruction; 89 involved in agriculture; 89 dealing with the elderly; 31 involved in demining/mine awareness, The Directory of Humanitarian and Development Agencies in Bosnia and Herzegovina, April 1999, p. vi.

[11] For outline and structure of common institutions, See list of appendices, No. 2.

[12] My field research undertaken in BiH indicated that the vast majority of citizens in both entities do *not* consider the Inter Entity Boundary Line to be a border.

[13] Societal security, in this sense, is interchangeable with emancipation, as indeed they are the same thing. Emancipation according to Ken Booth is the freeing of people from constraints such as war, poverty, poor education and political oppression. Emancipation is thus closely related to security, the security of the individual against war, poverty, poor education and political oppression.

[14] Constitution of Bosnia and Herzegovina, Article II: 5. Refugees and Displaced Persons.

[15] According to Peter Krale, European Community Monitoring Mission, Head of BiH Desk, a feeling of insecurity causes the slow progress in returns. For example 200,000 Serbs left Sarajevo after the signing of the Dayton Peace Accord and they do not feel secure enough as of yet to return to their homes. See list of appendices, No. 1.

[16] The above statistics have been taken from the annex to the Madrid Declaration of the Peace Implementation Council, Madrid, 16, December 1998.

[17] "Second Phase Returns" refer to where return of peoples to their pre-war home, involves the eviction of peoples, of a different ethnicity, who moved into that accommodation during or after the war. It is the most sensitive form of return, but necessary if ethnic cleansing is to be reversed. In 1998 there were 24 successful Serb evictions in Banja Luka, thus facilitating the return of the pre-war Muslim families. This information was acquired from Josc Maria Aranaz, Human Rights and Legal Officer, Office of the High Representative, Banja Luka, BiH. See list of appendices, No. 1.

[18] On July 2nd 1999 the Office of the High Representative made changes to property laws so as to improve the implementation of Annex 7 of the Dayton Peace Agreement. Such alterations are welcomed as the property issues is a major stumbling block preventing returns, according to Christopher Harland, Human Rights Officer, Office of the High Representative. See list of appendices, No. 1.

[19] Kristof Gosztonyi, RRTF, Mostar, suggested that RRTF could be wholly successful in five years if the International Community continue to uphold pressure and if donor money continues to be directed towards BiH. See list of appendices, No. 1.

[20] Figures attained from James Fergusson, Public Affairs Officer, OHR, Sarajevo. See list of appendices, No. 1.

[21] OHR Head Quarters, Sarajevo, Internal e-mail.

[22] See http://www.ohr.int/rrtf.htm 15th May 2000.

[23] According to Kristof Gosztonyi, RRTF, Regional Office South, political pressure and donor funding must continue if "phase two" returns are to continue successfully in the Mostar area.

[24] The leading political force in Croatia, the HDZ, gains much of its support from the Croats in canton 7, minority returns of Croats would have the effect of weakening support for the HDZ in this area.

[25] In the municipal elections (April 8th 2000) turnout was down by about 30% from 1997 in the Croat dominated municipality of Caplijina. The International Crisis Group maintain that the low turnout was caused by the fact that there was no way to register support for new moderate alternatives within the Bosnian Croat community following the victory of the democratic forces in Croatia (after the death of President Tudjman), other than by staying away from the polling booth, as moderate Bosnian Croat parties had neither the time nor the recourses to organise themselves following the capitulation of the HDZ in Croatia. See International Crisis Group, "Bosnia's municipal Elections 2000: Winners and Losers", April 27, 2000.

[26] In the first five months of 1999, 239 Bosniaks and 17 Bosnian Croats moved into RS. These statistics were taken from UNHCR Statistics Package.

[27] Ms. Sauelie Golubouid, Priority Return Officer, OSCE, Banja Luka, commenting on the return of elected officials. See list of appendices, No.1.

[28] Sanela Paripovic, Deputy Ombudsperson for BiH, believes that the office of the Ombudsperson is growing in stature and is quite successful. The Office of the Ombudsperson makes recommendations to the resident government. If the matter is not dealt with adequately at this level the case is transferred to the Chamber of Human Rights, whose decisions are binding. See list of appendices, No. 1.

[29] DPA, Annex 4, Article V, emphasis added.

[30] "Others" are Bosnians who are not Serbs, Croats or Bosniaks.

[31] International Crisis Group Report, "Changing the Logic of Bosnian Politics: Discussion Paper on Electoral Reform", 10 March, 1998, p. 5.

[32] It is generally agreed now that the elections were held too soon after the war had ended, being forwarded at the time as a panacea against the undemocratic evils that had emerged in the region. However because of the great tensions and hatred following the war, the 1996 elections amounted to a poor ethnic census, as political parties exclusively represented the narrow interests of their own ethnic group and not the entire electorate, Bosnian society thus remained polarised and politics degenerated into a "zero-sum" affair.

[33] The "anti-integration" ethos of the HDZ was articulated most dramatically by BiH Presidency member and HDZ party President, Ante Jelavic on 24 February 2000, when we called for the cancellation of the BiH Federation. Such a cancellation would effectively destroy the Dayton Peace Accord. See Official OHR Website, "OBN News Review", 24 February 2000. *http://www.ohr.int/issues00/p000224c.htm*

[34] Ambassador Robert Barry, Head of the OSCE Mission to BiH and Mr. Francois Froment-Meurice, the Chairman of the Election Law Commission, formally presented the draft Election Law to BiH parliamentary assembly officials on October 21 1999. It was intended that the draft be passed by BiH parliament before national elections in Autumn 2000. However, as that was not achieved, it was decided to implement the draft without the backing of the parliament for the November 2000 national elections.

[35] Julien Bertmoud Implementation Compliance Officer, OSCE, Mostar. See list of appendices, No. 1.

[36] This poll was carried out by the permanent election law information campaign in order to measure the attitudes of the public about the current election system of BiH and possible electoral reform. A total of 3,000 BiH citizens were interviewed, 1,000 interviews with Bosniaks in Bosniak majority areas in the federation; 1,000 interviews with Croats within the Croat majority areas in the federation; and 1,000 with Serbs in Republika Srpska.

[37] For example in the early 1990s during the Serb occupation of parts of the Krajina region of Croatia, the village of Pakrac in Western Slavonia was literally on the front line. The railway track running through the middle of the village represented the border of occupation. During this period, one half of the village had no water supply, while the other half was without electricity. A group of women from both sides of the village, including ethnic Serbs and Croats, came together to find ways to pool their resources in order to do the laundry. This group has stayed together and has grown into a highly organised NGO providing a variety of services to the local community. See Mulheir, Georgette and O' Brien, Tracey, "Private pain, public action: Violence against women in war and peace", *Centre for Peace and Development Studies*, University of Limerick, 1999.

[38] Official OSCE Website, "Women can do it seminars support women in politics" November 23, 1999.
http://www.oscebih.org/pressreleases/november1999/23-11-women.htm

[39] Out of Country Voting allows refugees' to post their votes to their pre-war constituency, thus allowing refugees a voice in the reconstruction of their country.

[40] The Provisional Election Commission is chaired by the OSCE Head of Delegation. Within its structure it also contains International Organisation representatives, representatives from the two entities (representatives are proposed by the prime Minister in both the Federation and RS), and independent representatives reflecting the views of society.

[41] It is hoped that the newly elected Council of Ministers will ratify the draft election law for the 2002 general and presidential elections. This is indeed very possible as the new Council of Ministers is moderate in make-up and its Chairman Dr. Bozidar Matic is moderate and pro-reform.

[42] I obtained this information by telephone interview with Sanela Becirovic (OSCE Deputy Spokesperson for BiH) on February 16th 2000.

[43] International Crisis Group, "Bosnia's Municipal Elections 2000: Winners and Losers", 27 April, 2000, p. 2.

[44] Already certain progress has been made in this regard as the troika Presidency expressed in their "New York Declaration" (United Nations Security Council, New York, 15 November 1999) *that they* intend "to seek improved inter-entity military co-operation, including through creation of joint units to participate in United Nations peacekeeping operations". See Office of the High Representative Website, "New York Declaration, New York", 15 November 1999, *http://www.ohr.int/nyd/en-19991115-a.html*

[45] From interviews conducted I found that one of the principal factors hindering the process of democratisation in BiH was the fact that people lacked the knowledge and capacity to construct and orientate policy at local and regional level.

[46] Human Development Report, Bosnia and Herzegovine Independent Bureau for Humanitarian Issues, Sarajevo, 1998, p. 20.

[47] Ibid., p. 43.

[48] Ibid., p. 45.

[49] List of appendices, No. 2.

[50] List of appendices, No. 2.

[51] Peter Krale, ECMM Headquarters, Sarajevo. See list of appendices, No. 1.

[52] See list of appendices, No. 2.

[53] For example municipality "Mostar Southwest" consists of 79.89% Croats, 14.78% Bosniaks, 3.69% Serb and 1.63% Others (UNHCR Statistics), 1999.

[54] The success of multi-ethnic and moderate political parties at the 2000 municipal elections should enhance political pluralism and greater representation.

[55] See list of appendices, No. 2.

[56] Morris Power, OHR, Sarajevo. See list of appendices, No. 1.

[57] Mr. Dzemal Subasic, list of appendices, No. 1.

[58] List of appendices, No. 4.

[59] The SLOGA coalition was a minority government consisting of the following political parties: The SNS (Leader Plavsic) who split from the SDS because of corruption allegations against Karadiz and other party members; The SPRS is a sister party to Milosevic's socialist party in Serbia although the links have become more tense and ambiguous since the Kosovo crisis 1999; the SNSD were the third biggest party in the coalition. They are linked to western/European social democratic parties (Leader Dodic, who was previous Prime Minister of RS). Both the SNSD and former Prime Minister Dodic represent a softening of attitude in RS, a clear departure from the post war "Pale" leaders. Dodic as Prime Minister was strongly supported by the international community (OHR). Two other small political parties made up the remainder of the coalition. This information was attained from Pasi Poysari, OHR Political Advisor, Banje Luka, BiH. See list of appendices, No. 1.

[60] *Ontopology*, the connection of "the ontological value of present-being to its *situation*, to the stable and presentable determination of a locality, the *topos* of territory, native soil, city, body in general". Derrida, Specters of Marx, in: Edkins, Jenny, Persram, Nalini and Pin-Fat, Veronique (eds.), *Sovereignty and Subjectivity* (London: Lynne Rienner Publishers, 1999), p. 27.

[61] Rather than creating a protectorate the International Community decided instead to allow the peoples of BiH to govern themselves. The OHR was created nevertheless so as to oversee the civil implementation of the GFAP. The peace agreement directs the High Representative to: Monitor implementation of the peace settlement; maintain close contact with the Parties to promote full compliance; co-ordinate the activities of the international organisations and agencies; provide guidance as appropriate to the International Police Task

Force; report periodically on progress. The High Representative is the final authority regarding interpretation of the Agreement on civilian implementation. According to the Agreement, the tasks of civilian implementation include: The establishment of political and constitutional institutions; economic reconstruction and the rehabilitation of infrastructure; promotion of respect for human rights; encouragement of return of displaced persons and refugees; continuation of humanitarian aid for as long as necessary; support for and assistance with the election process being supervised by OSCE.

[62] From my own observation I noted that the common passports do not succeed in hiding the ethnic affiliation of the passport holder, as the Bosnian Serb passports are written in Cyrillic, while the Bosniak and Croat passports are written in the Latin form. However the Troika Presidency stated in their New York Declaration (15 November 1999) that they are supporting the creation of a common passport carrying only the name of BiH on its cover in both Cyrillic and Latin scripts.

[63] The three members of the presidency of Bosnia and Herzegovina recommitted themselves to a sovereign multi-ethnic state while addressing the United Nations Security Council on November 15, 1999. In their "New York Declaration" the Presidency noted with great vigour that "anti-Dayton forces advocating ethnic hatred and division…have no place in the politics of Bosnia and Herzegovina". See Ibid.

[64] According to Jamers Fergusson, Public Affairs Spokesman, OHR. See list of appendices, No. 1.

[65] In fact the SCMM met on 3 November 1999 to discuss reducing the size of the Federation and RS militaries by 15% by the end of 1999, with another 15% reduction scheduled in the year 2000. See Barry Robert, 1999. OSCE Website "Report by head of mission Robert Barry to the Permanent Council of the OSCE", *http://www.oscebih.org/events/barry_report-10-12-99.htm*

[66] The commission even continued to function at the height of the NATO bombing in Kosovo.

[67] In May 2001 the official opening of a Muslim Mosque in Banja Luka was greeted with street violence by radical Serb elements. However, what is most noteworthy is that the great majority of Serb political parties and politicians renounced this violence, as the street violence was carried out by a small factional element, whose actions did not represent the majority of Serbs in RS. Nevertheless, the violence manifests that issues of identity are still potentially explosive in the region.

Chapter 6
Dayton: An Unbundling of Sovereignty

I now wish to analyse whether the post-Dayton implementation process actually signals an *unbundling* of state sovereignty and marks in some part the creation of dispersed forms of vertical and horizontal sovereignty. Realism defines security in a narrow sense, as explained in chapter two. From the realist point of view, "security is identified as identity, unity and an imposed order. Difference is a threat".[1] However, such realist definition of security, while it may impose security based upon order, does little in way to respond to the needs of human security and emancipation. Rather my aim is to critique how human emancipation might be created.[2] In achieving this objective binary opposition, upheld by the centralised state structure, must be deconstructed. In achieving this objective the creation of dispersed vertical and horizontal structures hold the ability to *unbundle* the modern notion of sovereignty/territoriality/identity and thus hold the key to our understanding of how contemporary spatial reorganisation might be pursued.[3] Contemporary spatial reorganisation does not necessarily require a complete deconstruction of the traditional constructs namely, sovereignty/territoriality/identity, but rather, on the contrary, it would appear that more partial and ambiguous changes would catalyse the diffusion of modernity constructs without clearly replacing them with "more modern bundled constructs", such as world government or micro-regionalism.

The embryonic transition therefore occurring in BiH marks a *transition* from modern to postmodern rather than an *elevation* from modern to more modern.[4] I am not attempting here to argue that the post-Dayton developments, outlined in the previous section, were in any manner consciously created by postmodern theorists, but rather were created as a response to the given "socio-political habitat". I coin this phrase, "socio-political habitat", as a response to Toulmin's calling to utilise biology as a starting point.[5]

Rather than creating new constructs with which to replace the old and thus attempting to locate a comprehensive system of theory with universal and timeless relevance, it may be more ambitious and feasible to simply respond to the socio-political habitat. As stated by Toulmin in his work *Cosmopolis* it may be more fitting to base a system upon the ethos of ecology. A system based upon the ethos of ecology could show more possibilities for diversity and change, locality and time. Such a process, by questioning the construct of the nation state, should allow the development of human emancipation. Evidently the process occurring in Post-Dayton BiH, is very much a specific response to the socio-political habitat created as a result of the war. In this manner, the process cannot be considered a formula on how to reconstruct a war-torn country, nor a consciously constructed post-modern manifestation, but as an individual response prompted by the specific environment.

The process underway in BiH, because of its responsiveness to the socio-political habitat, has the ability to respond to diversity and change, locality and time. It may achieve this objective through the unconscious[6] development of dispersed forms of horizontal and vertical sovereignty. In responding to the socio-political habitat, the articulation of realist driven policy was simply not compatible with the specific environment. The emphasis many realists place upon territory, power and monolithic identity and the means by which the three are tied together through the use of sovereignty within the realist mindset could and would only lead to fratricidal, ethno-national struggle in Bosnia.

If a realist agenda was to be implemented in BiH, a powerful centralised sovereign government, a strongly armed border and a ruling homogenous identity would ensue, meaning the abolition of the IEBL, cantons, entities and the institutionalised multi-ethnic ethos. The establishment of such a realist agenda would automatically create an environment where large sections of society must experience some form of alienation from power, identity and/or territory. Therefore, the implementing partners in Bosnia were left with no feasible choice but to respond to the socio-political habitat, and in doing so unconsciously deconstructed the traditional notion of sovereignty through the creation of dispersed vertical and horizontal structures. The talks at Dayton brought realist politician together, all in principal wanted their ethnicity to be enwrapped in the Westphalian model. To do so was impossible without mass population movement or ethnic cleansing, as all three ethnicities lived side by side in Bosnia. Dayton, therefore, was forced to respond to this socio-political habitat of enmeshed ethnicity, nations and religions and thus attempted to create responsive structures beyond the realms of the Westphalian model. The fact that Dayton does not model the quintessential nation state has caused many to view its construction as a failure, I view it as a theoretical signpost, although imperfect, as to how wars of the present may be responded to. Many political analysts also consider the implementation of Dayton a failure, as it has failed to centralise a government in Sarajevo. It is the case the common institutions created by Dayton have been ineffective due to the obstructionist policies of ethnonationalist parties. This is a fundamental problem for Dayton and must be overcome. However, we must also keep in mind that the potential benefit of Dayton arises from the fact that common institutions in Sarajevo, should only represent one of many vertical sovereign structures. The aim of the OHR should not be to create common institutions comparable to that of a Westphalian nation state. To do so can only lead to alienation of ethnicities and potential war. Rather all levels of vertical sovereignty codified in the *Dayton Peace Accord* must be supported and enhanced.

The Process of Spatial Reconfiguration

If we return again to the four principal factors outlined in the previous chapter, one sees how, and the extent to which, this process of dispersal is occurring. Previously, I critiqued the extent and mechanisms by which the return process is occurring. This return process theoretically should allow, unconsciously, for the creation and development of both dispersed horizontal and vertical forms of sovereignty. Firstly, the return process can allow for the incremental *creation* of a vertical dispersal of sovereignty. The liberation of identities and the creation of space can be constructed, in this sense, by the institutional structure which gives expression to all identities. The necessity of this derives from the fact that the human and economic cost of conflict is so great that we must attempt to develop mechanisms so as to prevent war. We must lessen the chance of conflict by constructing communities responsive to the needs of identities. This duty is most poignant in the case of BiH considering the recent war, where identities became devoured in fratricidal warfare. A form of dispersed vertical sovereignty can help construct communities responsive to the needs of identities, insofar as it allows all identities to articulate and represent themselves within a dispersed structure. Such a dispersal of sovereignty is clearly required in order to limit the preponderance of certain identities that claim to represent the whole. The institutional political structure created under Dayton theoretically allows for such a diffusion and overlapping of identities, with the establishment of municipalities, cantons, entity governments and common institutions. However, the effectiveness of such institutions, in practical terms, can only reach their potential if and when the return process is successfully completed.

The creation of institutional structures that represent peoples at all levels and within jurisdictions relevant to the task pursued can indeed create space and allow the expression of all identities. Because of the movement of peoples and ethnic cleansing carried out during and after the war in BiH, one finds that in many municipalities and cantons, one ethnicity has total preponderance. This reality obviously damages the potential effectiveness of the institutions, as they cannot be as responsive or multiple as they would otherwise be. The return process is therefore a huge priority, as it potentially can create multi-cultural, multi-ethnic constituencies and institutions that in turn should help create space.

A successful return process will also facilitate the development of dispersed horizontal sovereignty. The return of minorities specifically, demands the creation of dispersed horizontal structures so as to facilitate needs. As stated in chapter two horizontal sovereignty can best be created through the use of a functionalist approach. As functionalism has the ability to overcome the sovereign power of the nation state by constructing appropriate structures that are not territorially based, but based upon a need or duty, the theory has thus the ability to provide for minority returns. In this sense the theory of functionalism presents viable practical approaches to reconciliation. Minority returns (phase two returns) involve the return of citizens to an entity, canton or municipality where they are often physically or psychologically alienated from the political process and socio-economically disadvantaged. A prime example of this case scenario is the case of Serbs living in Sarajevo. Because the *Dayton Peace Accord* was a document hammered out under the threat of continued war and because all major parties involved were extremely ethno-national in character, it is the case that the *Accord* itself enshrines a certain ethno-national ethos. For example, Serb minorities returning to their pre-war homes within the Federation are in reality prevented from voting in the tripartite presidential elections, insofar as it is stipulated that the Bosniak and Croat members of the Presidency shall only be elected from within the Federation. Again at municipal, cantonal and national parliament level the slight numerical stature of Serbs within the Federation gives them a weak voice. As stated in the previous section, such alienation is at least partially overcome by the existence of common institutions, the representative nature of municipals and cantons due to their restricted size, plus the new election draft. However, in the immediate term, considering the failure of the political institutions, alienation is mainly overcome through the work of international and domestic humanitarian and developmental organisations that respond to human need and duty.

Dispersed Horizontal Sovereignty in Practice

I refer to this process as dispersed horizontal sovereignty, as people are given a sovereign voice at local "horizontal" level by functionalist institutions. I refer to horizontal sovereignty as "dispersed" insofar as functionalist organisations within various specialised fields provide a sovereign voice for the individual at local level, particularly for those alienated from the dispersed vertical structure. One such organisation, for example, "Demokratska inicijativa sarajevskih Srbska", the "Democratic Initiative of Sarajevo Serbs", helps provide Serbs living in Sarajevo with a sovereign voice at local level. They attempt to promote and protect human rights; create conditions for refugee return; provide health protection and build understanding and co-operation between different national communities. Organisations such as the Democratic Initiative of Sarajevo Serbs represents the type of organisation alluded to by Mitrany, when he spoke of peace being achieved through organisation around issues other than security as traditionally understood.

The work of ECHO is another example of how citizens can be empowered and thus given a sovereign voice. ECHO's mission in BiH has worked with the aim of building local capacity, which is why local procurement and the hiring and training of local staff have been among its priorities.[7] ECHO utilises specialised local national and international NGOs to implement projects. Such local NGOs because of their sensitivity to the local situation and their knowledge of the local environment tend to be highly successful. Again both ECHO and the implementing partners (NGOs) work closely with municipalities and cantons, as projects (particularly housing and return projects) demand their expertise, understanding and political will. The working relationship between ECHO and the indigenous political institutions helps to build local capacity, as local politicians experience the proven methods and procedures used by NGOs in establishing; for example, food, hygiene, social assistance, health, monitoring, rehabilitation and return. Such local capacity building is vital, as my research would show that one of the biggest issues preventing adequate governance in BiH is the lack of political experience and political know-how. Interestingly greater articulation of horizontal sovereignty will also have a positive effect upon dispersed vertical sovereignty, as it will help create a more multi-ethnic environment and subsequently greater human security.

The Nexus between Dispersed Horizontal and Vertical Institutions

It is evident that a nexus forms between both dispersed horizontal and vertical institutions, complementing each other and furthering emancipation. For example, regarding the issue of minority returns the RRTF co-operates with ECHO and NGOs as vehicles capable of fulfilling needs and duties at the local level,[8] whilst simultaneously co-ordinating with municipal and cantonal ministers, as returns are administered by municipal housing officers. A problem arises from the fact that, under the current electoral law, the political make-up of many municipalities tends to be quite nationalist in nature and, therefore, such municipalities often attempt to hinder minority returns. There are also more practical problems including lack of accommodation and double occupancy. Functionalist organisations such as ECHO and certain NGO's can utilise their positions so as to promote progress within municipalities and cantons, by providing required services in return for greater municipal co-operation with the RRTF.

Examining the issue of education one also locates a nexus between dispersed vertical and horizontal sovereignty. Within the Federation, for example, cantonal ministers legislate regarding education, whilst the federal educational ministry simply plays an advisory role. Whilst the OHR plays a significant role in attempting to promote multi-ethnic schooling,[9] functionalist organisations also play a significant part in helping bring about this goal. For example, an Italian NGO, Nuoevo Frontiera, established an educational programme within BiH so as to heighten awareness, whilst ECHO rehabilitated 165 schools between 1995-1998. This work is vital, as the development of a more inclusive and reflective educational system would have the effect of creating space by destroying the latent ethno-national contradictions.[10] This process is both arduous and complex, according to Fidelma Donlon, OHR human rights officer, Mostar,[11] as the cantonal and municipal elected representatives from different ethnicities in cantons 6 and 7 refuse to sit in the same chamber, making the development of a cohesive and inclusive education policy extremely difficult in that region. Therefore, until such time as more moderate politics prevail the work of institutions operating on the horizontal axis is fundamental. In this regard the work of institutions such as UNESCO[12] and the Catholic School Centre is helping create a more benign and inclusive educational environment is fundamental.

The development of functionalist organisations that put emphasis upon local capacity building is certainly having the effect of creating a dispersed form of horizontal sovereignty. This can be seen by the fact that there were 284 national NGOs in BiH in 1999, which accounted for 61% of humanitarian and developmental organisations in the country. Added to that much of the staff of international NGOs and other organisations are local, in this way supplying the local peoples with relevant experience and knowledge.

Existing Sectors of Non-Cooperation

It is evident that local capacity building is growing; however, organs within the horizontal sector cannot supply many primary requirements. For example, technical needs such as power, water and transport must be supplied, by nature of their character, at a national or indeed supra-national level. In post-war BiH there has been a total lack of co-operation and co-ordination on these fronts. Currently water and heating are supplied at cantonal level within the Federation,[13] whilst telecommunications is co-ordinated at entity level. The *Dayton Peace Accord* provided for the establishment of public corporations in such areas as utility, energy, postal and communication facilities (Annex 9). Unfortunately, these corporations are suffering from the same lack of co-operation that hamstrings the central institutions created by Annex 4. For example, the railway corporation has no real power, even though both entity ministers of transportation are on its board. To date it has been relatively unsuccessful. There is no regularly scheduled freight traffic between the entities. There is no regularly scheduled passenger service between the two entities, and the passenger line from Sarajevo to Ploce operates at a minimal level.

Annex 9 article III allows for the creation of utility, energy, postal and communication corporations. Although the federation and RS governments have been unwilling to create joint corporation for transmission of electric power, the three ethnically based state-owned power companies are beginning to work together. On October 28, 1998 the three Elektroprivredas formed a business association registered in Sarajevo, to co-ordinate the joint transmission of electrical energy. It is important that greater co-operation develops; otherwise greater material deprivation will ensue, conditioning the environment upon which nationalism could once again gain a fervent hold on society. The likelihood of public corporations, which provide such technical services, developing is totally dependent upon the development of more benign relations between the three ethnicities within the vertical institutional structure. Therefore, as in the case of annex IV, it is really only with the creation of more moderate multi-ethnic politics will we see the establishment of adequate public services. As stated previously, in order for this to occur, confidence-building measures must be established. Promoting the return of refugees, promoting electoral reform and enhancing the political structures can achieve this goal.

Unbundling Territorial Sovereignty[14]

In analysing the extent to which the political structures created under Dayton succeed in *unbundling* state-centred theory, one finds that the *unbundling* of sovereignty is caused by the dispersed horizontal and vertical structures. A dis-aggregation of power away from the centre through the use of various vertical and horizontal structures deconstructs state power. State power according to Michael Mann consists of regulations and means of coercion centrally administered and territorially bounded.[15] Mann maintains that power brings about the state's distinctive contribution to social life;[16] if power can therefore be reallocated and dispersed the state's contribution to social life will automatically become less important.

The dispersed vertical chain of sovereignty within BiH certainly has this potential. It is obvious that such potential has not been wholly realised as of yet because of the grip on power ethno-nationalist political parties still hold, however as stated previously, the new election draft should allow a more inclusive politics to develop, as the April 2000 municipal election results have certainly signalled. The development of more moderate and inclusive politics in BiH will not only positively affect the vertical institutions namely the relationship between local governance, entity governance and the common institutions but it will affect the dispersed horizontal institutions also in positive fashion. Less nationalist municipalities will benefit greatly, as both the international community and NGOs are eagerly willing to functionally support those municipalities that are promoting inclusion. The proper functioning of local governance together in co-operation with non-governmental functionalist institutions will help create human security. The dispersed vertical structure potentially may destroy the crystallisation of power, while the functionalist nature of the horizontal structure aids the empowerment of peoples at local level to challenge social problems. Such a deconstruction of sovereignty obviously theoretically challenges the traditional notion of the nation state and in this manner potentially should create the space necessary to provide *human security* when the issues outlined in chapter five are eventually redressed.

The Stature of the Inter Entity Boundary Line

A reconstitution of the sovereign nation state is required so as to place the security of peoples before that of borders and territoriality. In doing this, we must come to question state-centred theory, which controls and dictates both power and social forces. The development of dispersed vertical and horizontal structures in BiH, which devolve sovereignty away from the centre, signal an initial instigation in this process. An analysis of the current status of the Inter Entity Boundary Line (IEBL) separating Republika Srpska from the Federation is a clear example displaying the effect of *unbundled* sovereignty upon borders and territoriality. The GFAP created the IEBL, which ethno-nationalist parties on both sides envisaged to mark the beginnings of their ultimate aspiration. Large sections of Serb nationalists hoped, and indeed still hope, that the IEBL would overtime grow in stature eventually becoming a demarcated border, marking the birth of a Republika Srpska nation state. Such a development would be detrimental for *human security*, automatically creating an inside/outside dichotomy. Large sections of Bosniak nationalists willed the IEBL away and envisaged that the common institutions would over time become stronger, thus in reality withering the stature of the IEBL and thereafter creating a centralised BiH nation state. Of course, a concentration of power allied with the social ramification of such a development could only spell the re-emergence of ethno-nationalist warfare again in the region. Certain sections of Croat nationalism hoped, and still hope, to create a third entity within BiH. The creation of a third entity within BiH would in no manner create greater representation and rather would only allow ethno nationalists to promote the concept of ethnic demarcation, which again would result in fratricidal warfare.

The effective execution of dispersed vertical and horizontal sovereignty should have the effect of directing attention away from both borders and territoriality. However, as outlined in the previous chapter, there are a number of burning issues which up until now have prevented the development of sovereign dispersal. Nevertheless, over the past six years there has been some success in developing a dispersal of sovereignty. For example, from interviews conducted I found that the IEBL is generally not perceived as a border on either side of the line and it is obvious that both the continuation of the return process will further erode the actual territorial essence of the IEBL, whilst *not* symbolically removing it. The failings of ethno-nationalists to mould the IEBL to their own ends to date significantly manifests the degree to which the implementation process in BiH is moving away from state centric approaches. In order to consolidate this process a contonal system of governance needs to be introduced into RS. Considering the strength of the SDS in the RS parliament there is little chance that such a proposal would be excepted. Neither is a cantonal system for RS codified in the *Dayton Peace Accord,* meaning that the OHR have no mandate to implement such a system. However, more moderate political parties and personalities in RS must be made aware of the benefits of a cantonal system in RS, so that they might advocate it to the people. Firstly, it would lead to greater responsiveness, as the governance unit would be smaller and the cantonal assembly more reflective of the electorate in that area. Secondly, it would have the effect of aiding the development of moderate politics in the federation, as the great fear in the federation is that the RS national assembly is not representative of minority ethnicities. A cantonal system in RS would also assure the federation that the RS is part of Bosnia, such an assurance would have the effect of dampening the drive by the HDZ for Croat entity status.

Brcko Arbitration – Circumventing Spatiality

Even a more explicit manifestation of an emerging new spatial configuration, which marks in many respects a clear deconstruction of the traditional model of nation state, is found in the Brcko arbitration final award.[17] Brcko sits at the crossroads of Bosnia and Herzegovina where the narrowest portion of the Republika Srpska meets the Federation. The Posavina Corridor in the Republika Srpska, only five kilometres wide at Brcko, connects the eastern and western parts of the Republika Srpska and provides the easiest north-south access for the Federation across the Sava River to the rest of Europe. Traditionally the trade, industry and transport hub of the region, Brcko borders Croatia on the Sava and is within three hours of Zagreb and ninety minutes from Belgrade via Croatia. The 1991 population census shows that Brcko municipality consisted of 44% Bosniak, 25% Croat, 21% Serb and 10% other. Today, however, 45,000 of the 100,000 people living in the district are Serb, while 35,000 are Bosniak and 15,000 Croat. It is evident therefore that Serbs heavily ethnically cleansed Brcko during the war, the main victims being Bosniak. As a result of the war, the municipality has been split between the Federation and the RS and the town itself, situated north of the Inter Entity Boundary Line (IEBL), is 97.5% Serb, approximately 75% of whom are displaced persons from the Federation and Serb refugees from Croatia. At the Dayton Peace Talks in November 1995, the parties were unable to agree on control of Brcko. The dispute was put to international arbitration in Annex II of the *Dayton Peace Accords*.

On 14 February 1997, the Presiding Arbitrator of the Brcko Tribunal, Mr. Roberts Owen issued a decision placing the RS portion of the Brcko municipality under international supervision. The Tribunal further extended the supervision period, on 15 March 1998, for a year. The Final Award was ultimately issued on 5 March 1999. The Final Award creates a Special District for the entire pre-war *Opstina* whose territory belongs to *both Entities*, the Republika Srpska and the Federation. Ambassador Robert William Farrand was appointed as Brcko Supervisor at the Brcko Implementation Conference in Vienna on 7 March 1997. He has the responsibility of overseeing the implementation of the arbitration Final Award. From both a practical and theoretical perspective the most significant aspect of the Final Award is the fact that both entities can claim sovereignty over a unitary territory.

In this sense sovereignty is *not* based upon territory, borders, power or authority, as both entities simultaneously hold the district, whilst the district shall be internally and autonomously administered by a District authority. For example the statute of the Brcko district of BiH stipulates in article 3 that there shall be no flag and Coat-of-Arms for the district other than the flag and Coat-of-Arms of BiH. In this way neither entity can claim control over the region. In fact as outlined in article 9 the district administers most functions and powers autonomously. District residents may however choose and indeed change their entity citizenship, as stipulated in article 12.[18] The District authority comprising of a multi-ethnic, democratic Government shall govern all internal affairs. On 31 December 1997 a multi-ethnic police force also began operating in Brcko. In 1999 there were 120 Bosnian Serb, 20 Bosnian Croat and 90 Bosniak police officers in the Brcko police force.[19]

The Creation of Space in Brcko

The disregard for the traditional concept of nation state as sovereign authority both runs counter to idealist and realist/neo-realist approaches within IR theory and in fact can be critiqued in a postmodernist sense. Granting sovereign authority to one entity over the other could only result in conflict, as both entities laid claim to the Brcko region. Within the municipality the "other" identity would feel alienated, whilst the "we" identity would feel it necessary to asset "weness" so as to fend against the threat of "other". In granting both entities jurisdiction over the region whilst simultaneously creating a dispersed form of vertical sovereign authority within the region, and between the region and Sarajevo, the International Community has succeeded in "creating space" capable of accommodating all identities. The sovereign authority is vertical in the sense that a "connective tissue" will link the multi-ethnic Brcko government with the common institutions in Sarajevo regarding issues of common concern and issues that lie outside the realm of the Brcko district authority. The "connective tissue" will also run to the level of grassroots, insofar as the district government shall co-operate and liase with local functionalist institutions.

However, it is simply not enough to "create space" through the establishment of vertical sovereign authority, as such accommodation does not necessarily provide *human security*. In providing *human security* a functionalist alternative is required. The establishment of horizontal sovereignty helps provide such emancipation. If one examines areas within the Brcko arbitration zone, the lack of human emancipation is manifest. For example, the OHR has estimated that although 3,200 Bosniaks and 1,250 Croats have returned to Brcko town, which would signify a growing sense of spatial inclusion, societal impoverishment remains high. For example, 2,963 houses are without electricity. Regarding water supply, "the supply is sporadic, not potable, sewerage is in a state of disrepair".[20] Industry in the town is operating at 10-20% of pre-war levels. However, a number of NGOs and International Organisations are helping the people rebuild. In this regard ECHO, Norwegian peoples aid, Swiss Disaster Relief, UNHCR and World Vision are helping provide for local peoples. Such functionalist institutions represent a horizontal form of sovereignty, in the manner in which they subtract power away from the centre and supply local people with a voice, by responding to their needs and through the development of services and functions.

Conclusion: A Summation of Post-Dayton Implementation

Bosnia and Herzegovina will face many colossal challenges if the General Framework Agreement for Peace is to deliver a lasting peace. Within the previous chapter I have pointed to the "burning issues" within post-Dayton Bosnia that condition both the environment and the implementation process concurrently. These issues are paramount, insofar as they hold the ability to deconstruct sovereignty, "soften" identity and create space. As stated above such a process is necessary, as the traditional notion of sovereignty cannot respond to the challenges, which Bosnia holds. The *unbundling* of sovereignty, therefore, signals in many respects a new departure in International Relations theory, capable of countering the realist model. The alternative to the realist model of centralised state sovereignty is based upon the creation of a vertical and horizontal form of sovereignty. If, however, such an alternative is to be viable in Bosnia and Herzegovina, the "burning issues" critiqued in the previous chapter must be positively addressed. The importance and complexity of these factors were uncovered through primary research. *Election reform* is one such issue that holds the ability to create a more inclusive, multi-ethnic BiH. Specifically the incorporation of the new electoral draft should allow the development of moderate politics, thus facilitating the effectiveness of both dispersed vertical and horizontal sovereignty. *The return of refugees and displaced persons (DPs)* is cardinal to unbundling sovereignty and thereby unlocking peace in the region. Specifically progress regarding minority returns is monumental, insofar as minority returns aid the dissolution of state centred preponderance and allows the institutional framework created under Dayton to operate in a representative fashion. From the research undertaken it would seem that minority returns are likely to increase rather than decrease with time.

Humanitarian and developmental organisations further condition this process of emancipation. The involvement of local developmental organisations, run by local people, plus the International Community's support for municipalities and local enterprises is helping create a culture of self-help. The ethos of development from below has also gained credence within the institutional structure of BiH, and in the long term the creation of representative and decentralised political institutions should be able to become more responsive to social challenges. Having outlined the principal factors unique to BiH which hold the ability to dis-aggregate authority away from the centre, this chapter proceeds to augment the degree in which such developments mark an *unbundling* of sovereignty and signals in some part the creation of dispersed forms of vertical and horizontal sovereignty. To this end, I examine the extent to which the new election draft may create a more inclusive politics, by subduing ethno-national political parties. Such progress would invariably allow both the dispersed vertical and horizontal structures operate in a more cohesive manner. The return process would also allow for the true creation of a vertical dispersal of sovereignty, insofar as a successful return process would create multi-ethnic constituencies and thus create multi-ethnic vertical institutions.

The accommodation of identities is further enshrined by the *institutional political structure* which both allows for a clear diffusion of power, and facilitates the expression of dispersed horizontal sovereignty by way of local government institutions. Dispersed horizontal sovereignty is even further cultivated by functionalist organisations, which put emphasis upon local capacity building. The deconstruction of state/sovereignty brought about by a dispersal of vertical and horizontal sovereignty is manifest vividly by two significant developments in BiH. The failings of ethno-nationalists to mould the IEBL to their own ends manifest the degree to which the implementation process in BiH is moving away from state centric approaches. Even a more explicit manifestation of this reality, which marks in many respects a clear deconstruction of the traditional model of nation state, is located in the Brcko arbitration final award.

Within this chapter, I have identified the means by which the initial phasing of dispersed vertical and horizontal sovereignty is taking place in BiH. It is evident that the process is still very much at an initial stage. It would seem, however, that the ethnic complexity and political sensitivity in the country would continue to demand such an approach, as regression into politics based upon territory and borders can only lead to conflict.

Notes

[1] Dalby, Simon, *Creating the Second Cold War* (London: Pinter Publishers, 1990), pp. 167.
[2] Booth, Ken, "Security and Emancipation", *Review of International Studies*, Vol. 17, No. 4, p. 319.
[3] "The terrain of unbundled territoriality [...] is the place wherein a rearticulation of international political space would be occurring today". See Ruggie, 1993, in: Anderson, J., Brook, C. and Cochrane, A. (eds.), *A Global World?* (Oxford: The Open University, 1995), p. 109.
[4] From interviews conducted with the International Community, I found that most criticism of post-Dayton developments in Bosnia tended to revolve around the fact that what is being created in BiH does not replicate the modern notion of nation state, based upon state centralism, sovereign authority, territoriality, but instead deviates from such

rational/ethnocentric approaches in response to the "socio-political habitat". Much of the criticism, therefore, stems from the fact that post-Dayton structures negate against attempts to create a Westphalian modelled nation state.

[5] See Toulmin, Op cit.

[6] I use the word "unconscious" here, as it was never meditated that a form of dispersed horizontal and vertical sovereignty should be formed, rather the decentralised nature of Dayton and the evolution of post-Dayton functional structures in BiH, founded upon the complexity of the socio-political habitat, *unconsciously* created a dispersal of sovereignty.

[7] This information was given by Danelli Cavini, Information Officer, ECHO, Sarajevo. See list of appendices, No. 1.

[8] ECHO funded the building of 5,693 houses so as to facilitate the return process in 1998.

[9] The OHR have forced education ministers to proceed with educational reform. According to Claude Kiefer, Senior Educational Officer, OHR, it was hoped that all offensive materials would be removed from the curricula by the beginning of the school year 1999. See list of appendices, No. 1.

[10] Multi-ethnic schools are beginning to develop in BiH, specifically the Catholic School Centres, which are placed throughout the federation. In the Sarajevo Catholic School Centre for example, 50% of students are Croats; 40% of students are Bosniak; 9% of students are Serb and 1% of students belong to the International Community.

[11] Fidelma Donlon, Human Rights Officer, OHR Mostar. See list of appendices, No. 1.

[12] UNESCO have recently compiled a report (Sept. 1999) on how best to develop an integrative curricula, capable of representing all ethnicity's and interests.

[13] Within the former Yugoslavia heating and electricity were operated at federation level, therefore the break up of the federation invariably caused a disintegration of the federal grid.

[14] The concept of unbundling sovereignty refers to the alterations to the traditional notion of territorial sovereignty, caused by pressures on the state from above and below, see Anderson, James, *et al*, Op cit., p. 97.

[15] Mann, 1986, in: Sjolander, Claire Turenne and Cox, Wayne S. (eds.), *Beyond Positivism Critical Reflections On International Relations* (London: Lynne Rienner Publishers, 1994), p. 165.

[16] Ibid.

[17] I spent a two-week period in the town of Brcko carrying out interviews, so as to assess the viability of the District plan announced on March 5th 1999. See list of appendices, No. 3.

[18] Statute of the Brcko district of Bosnia and Herzegovina, 7 December 1999, OHR publication.

[19] Figures supplied by the International Police Task Force, Brcko.

[20] Information supplied by International Police Task Force in Brcko, who have compiled town status reports in the Brcko region.

Chapter 7
Conclusion: Bridging Binary Opposition

It was when the ideal of the nation-state started to replace the idea of the multinational empires that war came to the Balkans. The carving out of national territories was a cumbersome process in other parts of Europe too, but in no other part was it so complicated, bloody and bordering on the impossible as in the Balkans mosaic. The idea of nation-state fitted extremely badly with the realities of the region. Thus, the 'powder keg' of the Balkans was born, and the practice of ethnic cleansing was initiated to create solid national areas.[1]

Within the discipline of International Relations theory, we encounter the rational approach of the modernity project, particularly in the works of realist and idealist theorists.[2] Kenneth N. Waltz's work *Man the State and War* is a clear example of this rational approach. We must come to question the essence of rationality, not necessarily rejecting it, as it plays such a colossal and integral part in the formulation of International Relations. International Relations must learn, however, to question one single, coherent, timeless logic and instead attempt to humanise itself. "…Democracy demands new post-nation-state institutions and new attitudes more attentive to the direct responsibility people bear for their liberties."[3] In achieving this objective a system must be forwarded which shows more possibilities for diversity and change, locality and indeed an awareness of time. In designing such a system we must come to question the nation state, which tends to paralyse any possible reformulation of International Relations.

A questioning of the nation state appears to open the door to possible solutions for post-cold war conflict. Considering, for example, that state alignment and consolidation augmented conflict in the former Yugoslavia, it becomes clear that a deconstruction of the state rather than a strengthening of the state structure may hold the answer. Promoting the deconstruction of the state structure and conditioning a reconfiguration of political space and identity in line with emancipation has made this book somewhat postmodern in character.

128

In the words of Lyotard: "We have paid a high enough price for the nostalgia of the whole and the one, [nation states]...Let us wage a war on totality; let us be witnesses to the unpresentable; let us activate the difference."[4]

The Changing Face of Sovereignty

Within chapter three the fundamental point is made that the idea of the modern nation state is dialectically connected to the idea of sovereignty. It was not really until the late medieval era and particularly the Renaissance that we see the development of sovereignty as a concept. Within this period the anachronistic structure of the medieval age was replaced by a multitude of thriving republics and principalities. Although we begin to see a glimpse of the modern state, sovereignty (authority) still resided with the King. There was also little or no consciousness of the concept of state, as there was less an emphasis upon a spatially demarcated territory and more an emphasis upon the vertical relationship between God, the King and the subjects. However, this was to change in the Classical period, as the idea of sovereignty was conditioned by a new mode of scientific knowledge. From this period onward the sovereign nation, defined in a spatial sense, has governed the character of International Relations. Whereas both in Classical times and Modernity there appears to be a strong link between the state and sovereignty, the character of this sovereignty differs considerably in both eras. In Classical times sovereignty was personified by a strong leader, be he monarch or otherwise. Within modernity the concept of sovereignty takes on a new meaning and is no longer personified. Instead the idea of the nation gives sovereignty the legitimacy it requires to structure a state. In this regard, no longer did God represent the epicentre of all authority, but now the nation, as the legitimate vehicle of the people, became the centre of authority. In creating a nation of identity, difference and otherness are excluded and indeed oftentimes augmented so as to give a greater sense of legitimate identity to the nation and it's peoples. Ironically the particularity of the outside is very much called upon so as to manifest the particularity of the inside. Within this dualism we may locate the essence of human insecurity.

Deconstructing Binary Opposition

Emphasis upon state-centric territoriality must be overcome if we are to respond to human insecurity. Both blurring the borders and putting greater emphasis upon the local can achieve this. In this sense we must take domestic/private/local space seriously in a way that mainstream IR analysis has never done before. Such a process involves deconstructing the identity-inside versus difference-outside dichotomy, which serves to maintain the structured hierarchy that pays reverence to the nation state. In clarifying the manner in which the identity versus difference dichotomy maintains the prevalent hierarchies, the enigma of otherness plays a vital role. Connolly elaborates upon the enigma of otherness, using Nietzsche's example of eternal damnation. "Once this thought becomes fixed in belief, the thought about what "eternal salvation" or "heaven" could mean becomes immunized against self-critical thought."[5] This same rational applies within International Relations, as the though of insecurity-instability puts the hierarchical status of the nation state beyond question. In attempting to deconstruct the enigma of otherness, it is an imperative to invert the hierarchy of identity, which serves to formulate otherness. In this sense the cleft between identity and difference must be bridged in order to create *human security*, or create what Bill McSweeney refers to as ontological security.

> Ontological security relates to the self, its social competence, its confidence in the actor's capacity to manage relations with others. It is a security of social relationship, a sense of being safely in cognitive control of the interaction context. It is relational at the most basic level of interaction: that of the mutual knowledge which is a condition of action, and which derives from a sense of *shared* community.[6]

Reconstituting Sovereignty

By way of response to the failings of the nation state, a broad *theoretical formula* is development in chapter two. In presenting an escape from ethno-nationalism, the creation of a vertical dispersal of sovereignty is introduced as a means of "softening identities" through the creation of overlapping identities and multiple spaces. With the "decoding" of identity the creation of a true form of dispersed horizontal sovereignty, capable of responding to human responsibility is made feasible. Such a process reduces the pertinence of nationalism, by preventing the nation state from manipulating nationality, religion or ethnicity as tools in maintaining its preponderance. This step towards a broadly functional alternative provides for the development of a multiplicity of spaces and times, capable of eroding the strictly demarcated nation state. The adoption of this theoretical model provides a viable means of overcoming wars based upon ethnicity, territory, borders and identity, in other words, nationalistic wars. The theoretical formula developed is thus ultimately capable of delivering *human security*. Such an approach involves the deconstruction of sovereignty as traditionally understood (within modernity), as the acceptance of sovereign territorial space gives rise to the inside/outside; identity versus difference dichotomy. There is thus a necessity that we redefine the character and essence of sovereignty, in the will to provide *human security* capable of incorporating all identities. In achieving this objective the theoretical formula is applied to the case of post-Dayton Bosnia and Herzegovina. The creation of such structures in BiH would have the effect of institutionalising duty and obligation and thereby establishing a more pro-active and responsive society. "To re-create civil society on this prescription does not entail a novel civic architecture; rather, it means reconceptualizing and repositioning institutions already in place."[7] Ultimately the aim is to respond to human responsibility by creating institutions in tune with the given socio-political habitat, so a to instill a true sense of *human security*.

The Case of Bosnia

A region such as Bosnia, based upon such religious and cultural diversity, was unquestionably vulnerable to explosive nationalism. The vulnerability became all the more intense because of the dire state of the economy from the 1970s onwards. Finally, with the dissolution of the Yugoslav federation in 1990, the full extent of ethno-nationalism was unleashed. With the dissolution of the League of the Communists of Yugoslavia, multiparty elections took place in each of the six Yugoslav republics in 1990. The Bosnian elections were held in November of 1990 and manifested the degree of ethno-national awareness in the region. Bosnia had never been a hot-bed of fervent nationalism. Conflict between local Muslim elites and the peoples of Bosnia in the past had been fuelled by social and economic factors. However, just as in the past, outside forces with powerful ambition attempted to take advantage of Bosnia. Bosnia thus fell victim to a barbaric fratricidal struggle, which endured for four years. Finally the *Dayton Peace Accord* brought the war to a halt. The Accord may have ended the war, but did not necessarily create peace. The Serbs in Republika Srpska (RS) felt aggrieved, as they had lost Sarajevo, and in its place had gained large spans of destitute land. Muslims and Croats felt they had lost the war as well, as RS had gained 49% of the territory and received entity status.

It was and continues to be an imperative that the structures created by the *Dayton Peace Accord* respond to such aggravations. On a theoretical level, the creation of a lasting peace depends largely upon the ability of the post-Dayton implementation process to create human security.[8] In this sense the success of post-Dayton implementation depends largely upon its ability to create a dispersal of sovereignty. It is argued within chapter six that this process it already underway, being aided by the continual return of refugees,[9] the development of multi-layered political institutions, the bottom up approach promoted by non-governmental organisations and the impending implementation of the new election laws. Such a process, by questioning the construct of the nation state, should allow the development of human emancipation. The post-Dayton implementation process is very much a specific response to the socio-political habitat created as a result of the war. This process, because of its responsiveness to the socio-political habitat, has the potential ability to respond to diversity and change, locality and time. It is the case that progress has been painstakingly slow; it is the case that the International Community have made misjudgements over the last six years; it is the case that the *Dayton Peace Accord* has flaws (the fact that there are no cantons in RS for example); it is the case that nationalism is still strong in Bosnia, the establishment of an illegal Croat parliament by the HDZ in Mostar in March 2001 being an obvious example. Nevertheless, a slow peace is growing in Bosnia. The dispersal of sovereignty on both a vertical and horizontal axis is operational, although problematic. "The Dayton accords, to this day, satisfy none of the noisy ultranationalists that claim to represent Bosnia's Muslims, Serbs and Croats. But they do win the support of the multiethnic majority in Bosnia and Herzegovina, as indicated by the landmark election last November that brought to power the country's first non-nationalist government. And implementation of the accords may serve as a model for fractured societies like Macedonia."[10] Dayton a model must be improved upon and refined. However, its basic theoretical essence, which both deconstructs the Westphalian state model and disperses sovereignty, represents a means by which to create the space necessary to provide *human security*.

The World is Fluid and about to be Remade

The process of analysis and inquiry undertaken within this book marks a clear discontinuity with traditional theories of International Relations. The modern system of state approach to International Relations is held under scrutiny and new configurations are elaborated upon as opposing regimes of truth capable of resolving the inadequacies in the modern system. As stated by John Gerard Ruggie (in relation to the possible development of postmodern configurations), "we lack even an adequate vocabulary; and what we cannot describe, we cannot explain".[11] Ruggie appears to be making the point that International Relations whilst, in theory, it promotes new and welcome departures, nevertheless fails to adequately create a constructive lexicon. Within this work, I have endeavoured to create a specialised lexicon capable of illuminating the means and manner by which alternative configurations might occur.

The coinage of specialised vocabulary namely, *dispersed vertical and horizontal structures*, helps illuminate the means by which I propose that territoriality, as comprehended within modernity, may be imploded. The analysis undertaken of post-Dayton Bosnia and Herzegovina displays the degree to which the traditional notion of territoriality is being practically reconstituted. I have endeavoured to theoretically explain and practically outline such new spatial configuration. Bosnia and Herzegovina is territorially relatively fixed, comprising an agreed and internationally recognised boarder. Nevertheless post-Dayton Bosnia enshrines a sense of territory within its structure, which is *not mutually exclusive*. Of course, the archetype of nonexclusive territorial rule is medieval Europe and, therefore, we may be witnessing the embryonic evolution of neo-medievalism. "The spatial projection of the medieval system of rule was structured by a nonexclusive form of territoriality, in which authority was both personalised and parcelised within and across territorial formations and for which inclusive bases of legitimation prevailed."[12]

Post-Dayton Bosnia in many respects reflects such a structure, with both the creation of dispersed vertical and horizontal forms of sovereign authority, which transcend the Inter Entity Boundary Line (IEBL), between the nation of Republika Srpska and the Federation of Croats and Muslims. Such an unbundling of territoriality/sovereignty stands at the cutting edge of International Relations today and indeed has relevance for the disciplines of comparative politics, development studies, security policy and conflict resolution. Therefore, the case of post-Dayton Bosnia, as imperfect and incomplete as the project may be, signals the means and manner by which the world is about to be remade.

Re-setting the Agenda of International Relations

It is time to re-set the agenda of International Relations in both a theoretical and practical sense. The emphasis IR has placed upon "building blocks" such as state sovereignty, nationalism and power has limited the structural equations that may be configured. If we are to truly respond to the purpose of International Relations, we must learn to theoretically and practically deconstruct, as with deconstruction comes the ability to re-formulate in accordance to need and responsibility.

Tackling contemporary conflict demands that we create the world. *Real politik*, balance of power and self-interest have for too long prevented practitioners and analysts within the field of IR from questioning the essence of conflict. Within this work the essence of conflict has been scrutinised in a holistic manner. The unitary nation state, which is served and instituted by a particular conception of sovereignty, drives binary opposition, resulting in human insecurity. Fundamentally, this book addresses the means by which binary opposition can be understood and bridged. On a broader level the essence of this question is fundamental, as many aspects of modernity appear entrapped within dichotomy. Within this book a theoretical structure is presented as a means of sublimation between the "us" and "them" dichotomy. In real terms the theoretical model aims to create multiple identity membership with a strong needs-based orientation. The theoretical model is practically applied to the intra-state Bosnian war (1991-1995), as the Bosnian conflict was created by binary oppositions, which both conditioned and segmented identities (be they religious, cultural, political, economical).

Representation of identity together with a responsiveness to need is presented within this work as a means by which human security can be ascertained. Developments in post-Dayton Bosnia and Herzegovina, within the last six years, attest to this philosophy. The local municipal elections held in April of 2000 and the November 2000 national elections in Bosnia and Herzegovina signalled that at least partially the sentiments of ethno-nationalism are abating and being replaced by a sense of inclusion. It would seem, therefore, that a deconstruction of the axiomatic "building blocks", in both a practical and theoretical sense, and their replacement with a sense of human security based upon responsiveness and representation should signal at least a partial re-setting of the IR agenda.

Notes

[1] Bildt, Carl, *Peace Journey: the struggle for peace in Bosnia* (London: Weidenfeld and Nicolson, 1998), p. 371.

[2] The two distinctively modern programs for mastering International Relations are deeply implicated in this project of modernity: realist balance of power thinking and idealist institutionalism, both of which have their origins in the eighteenth century. See Ruggie, John Gerard, (1993) "Territoriality and beyond: problematizing modernity in international relations", *International Organization*, Vol. 47, No. 1.

[3] Barber, Bemjamin and Suhulz, Andrea (eds.), *Jihad versus McWorld: How Globalism and Tribalism are reshaping the world* (New York: Ballantine Books, 1996), p. 277.

[4] Lyotard, Jean-Francois, *The Postmodern Condition*, in: Ruggie, John Gerard (1993) "Territoriality and Beyond: Problematizing Modernity in International Relations", *International Organization*, Vol. 47, No. 1, p. 145.

[5] Connolly, William, E. *Identity and Difference in Global Politics*, in: Der Derian, James and Shapiro, Michael, J. (eds.), *International/Intertextual Relations* (New York: Lexington Books, 1989), p. 332.

[6] McSweeney, Bill, *Security, Identity and Interests, A Sociology of International Relations* (Cambridge: Cambridge University Press, 1999), p. 157.

[7] Barbey, Benjamin, Op cit., p. 287.

[8] "There have always been two major components of human security: freedom from fear and freedom from want. This was a recognised right from the beginning by the United Nations. But later the concept was tilted in favour of the first component rather than the second." See Dalby, Simon, "Geopolitical Change and Contemporary Security Studies: Contextualizing the Human Security Agenda", Institute of International Relations, University of British Columbia, Working Paper, No. 30, April, 2000.

[9] Serbs are returning to the to their pre-war homes in Sarajevo at an accelerating pace. To date, 20,000 Serbs have returned to the capital Sarajevo, most in the past 18 months. Although the return process creates accommodation problems and certain hostilities, the accelerated pace of the process marks the slow but certain rebirth of multi-ethnic tolerance. See Whitaker, Raymond, "Homecoming Serbs bring New Heartache to Sarajevo", *The Independent on Sunday*, July 16, 2000, p. 19.

[10] Petritsch, Wolfgang, "Balkan Progress Is Real, So Don't Walk Away Now", *The International Herald Tribune*, March 26, 2001.

[11] Ruggie, John Gerard, *Constructing the World Polity* (London: Routledge, 1998), p. 175.

[12] Ibid., p. 179.

Bibliography

Acton, Lord, *Mapping the Nation* (London: Verso Press, 1996).

Agnew, John and Corbridge, Stuart, *Mastering Space* (London: Routledge, 1995).

Albrow, Martin, *The Global Age* (Cambridge: Polity Press, 1996).

Allcock, John, *Conflict in Former Yugoslavia, An Encyclopaedia* (Oxford: Oxford University Press, 1998).

Anderson, J., Brook, C. and Cochrane, A. (eds.), *A Global World?* (Oxford: The Open University, 1995).

Archibugi, D., Held, D. and Kohler, M., *Re-imagining Political Community* (Cambridge: Polity Press, 1998).

Ashley, K. Richard, "Untying the Sovereign State: A Double Reading of the Anarchy Problematique", *Millennium*, Vol. 17, No. 2, 1988.

Ashworth, Lucian, M., *David Mitrany, the functional approach and international conflict management*, Ottawa: The Norman Paterson School of International Affairs, No. 9, 1995.

Ashworth, Lucian, M., "The Roots of Westphalia: Patriarchal Conservatism in the Construction of Modern International Relations", Waterford: Political Studies Association of Ireland, 1997.

Ashworth, Lucian, M., "The Great Detour: Toxic Modernity and the Emergence of International Relations", Paper presented at the 23rd conference of the British International Studies Association, University of Sussex, 14-16 December, 1998.

Ashworth, Lucian, M., *Creating International Studies Angell, Mitrany and the Liberal Tradition* (Aldershot: Ashgate, 1999).

Ashworth, Lucian, M. and Keane, Rory, "Creating Wastelands Called Peace: The Failure of State Security and the Functionalist Alternative", International Political Science Association, XVIII World Congress, Quebec, 1-5 August, 2000.

Ashworth, Lucian, M. and Long, David (eds.), *New Perspectives on International Functionalism* (Basingstoke: Macmillan Press, 1999).

Axelrod, Robert, "The Dissemination of Culture", *The Journal of Conflict Resolution*, Sage Periodicals Press, April, Vol. 41, No. 2, 1997.

Axtmann, Roland, *Liberal Democracy into the Twenty-First Century* (Manchester: Manchester University Press, 1996).

Ball, Terence, *Transforming Political Discourse* (Oxford: Basil Blackwell Press, 1988).

Banac, Ivo, *The National Question in Yugoslavia* (Ithaca: Cornell, 1984).

Barbey, Bemjamin and Suhulz, Andrea (eds.), *Jihad versus McWorld: How Globalism and Tribalism are Reshaping the World* (New York: Ballantine Books, 1996).

Bartelson, Jens, *A Genealogy of Sovereignty* (Cambridge: Cambridge University Press, 1995).

Baudrillard, Jean (Mark Poster (ed.)), *Selected Writings* (Cambridge: Polity Press, 1988).

Baylis, John and Rengger, Nick (eds.), *Dilemmas of World Politics: International issues in a changing world* (Oxford: Oxford University Press, 1992).

Beardsworth, Richard, *Derrida and the political* (London: Routledge, 1996).

Beer, Francis, A. and Hariman, R., *Post-Realism-the rhetorical turn in IR* (East Lansing: Michigan State University Press, 1996).

Bennett, Christopher, *Yugoslavia's Bloody Collapse* (London: Hurst and Company, 1995).

Bhabha, Homi, K., *The Location of Culture* (London: Routledge, 1994).

Bhabha, Homi, K. (ed.), *Nation and Narration* (London: Routledge, 1990).

Bildt, Carl, *Peace Journey, The struggle for peace in Bosnia* (London: Weidenfeld and Nicholson, 1998).

Billig, Michael, *Banal Nationalism* (London: Sage Publications, 1995).

Bloom, William, *Personal Identity, National Identity and International Relations* (Cambridge: Cambridge University Press, 1990).

Booth, Ken, "Security and Emancipation", *Review of International Studies*, Vol. 17, No. 4, 1991.

Booth, Ken, *New thinking about strategy and International security* (London: Harper Collins Academia, 1991).

Booth, Ken, "Security and Self Reflections of a Fallen Realist", Toronto: YCISS Occasional Paper Number 26, 1994.

Booth, Ken and Smith, Steve, *International Relations Theory Today* (Cambridge: Polity Press, 1995).

"Bosnia-Herzegovina's English Language Newspaper", *The BiH reader*, June, 1999.

Bowie, Malcolm, *Lacan* (Cambridge: Harvard University Press, 1991).

Breuilly, John, *Nationalism and the state* (Manchester: Manchester University Press, 1993).

Brown, Chris, *International Relations Theory, New Normative Approaches* (New York: Harvester Wheatsheaf, 1992).

Brown, Chris, *Understanding International Relations* (New York: St. Martin's Press, 1997).

Bull, Hedley, *The Anarchical Society: A study of order in world politics* (Basingstoke: Macmillan Press, 1977).

Burchill, S. and Linklater, A., *Theories of International Relations* (Basingstoke: Macmillan Press, 1996).

Buzan, Barry, *People, States, and Fear – The national security problem of IR* (Brighton: Harvester Press, 1983).

Campbell, David, *Writing Security-US foreign policy and the politics of identity* (Manchester: Manchester University Press, 1992).

Carr, E. H., *The Twenty Years' Crisis* (New York: Harper and Row Publishers, 1964).

Centre of legal assistance for Women, "I'm back, and what to do now?", *Guide for Refugees 2*, Zenica, 1998.

Chandler, David, *Bosnia, Faking Democracy after Dayton* (London: Pluto Press, 1998).

Chirot, Daniel and Barkey, Karen, "States in Search of Legitimacy", *International Journal of Comparative Sociology*, Vol. XXIV, 1983.

Clark, Samuel, *State and Status* (Montreal and Kinston: McGill-Queen's University Press, 1995).

Claude, Inis, *Swords into plow shares* (New York: Random House, 1984).

Coakley, John, *The Territorial Management of Ethnic Conflict* (London: Frank Cass Publishers, 1993).

Coakley, John (ed.), *The Social Origins of Nationalist Movements* (London: Sage Publications, 1992).

Cochran, Molly, "Postmodernism, ethics and international political theory", *Review of International Studies*, Vol. 21, No. 2, 1995.

Cochrane, Allan, *Whatever Happened to Local Government?* (Buckingham: Open University Press, 1993).

Cohen, Mitchell and Fermon, Nicole (eds.), *Princeton Readings in Political Thought* (New Jersey: Princeton University Press, 1996).

Cohen, Ronald and Service, Elman, R., *Origins of the State* (Philadelphia: Institute for the Study of Human Issues, 1978).

Connolly, W., *Identity/Difference: Democratic Negotiations of Political Paradox* (New York: Ithaca University Press, 1991).

Couloumbis, Theodore and Wolfe, *Introduction to International Relations Power and Justice* (New Jersey: Prentice-Hall, Inc., 1982).

Cox, Robert, W., "Social forces, states and world orders: beyond international relations theory", *Journal of International Studies: Millennium*, Vol. 10, No. 2, 1981.

Cranna, Michael (ed.), *The true cost of conflict* (London: Earthscan Publications Ltd, 1994).

Cressy, David, *Education in Tudor and Stuart England* (London: Edward Arnold, 1975).

Dalby, Simon, *Creating the second Cold war* (London: Pinter Publishers, 1990).

Dalby, Simon, *Contesting an essential concept: Dilemmas in contemporary security discourse* (Ottawa: The Norman Paterson School of International Affairs, No. 6, 1994).

Dalby, Simon, "Geopolitical Change and Contemporary Security Studies: Contextualizing the Human Security Agenda", Institute of International Relations, University of British Columbia, Working paper, No. 30, April, 2000.

Dann, Otto and Dinwiddy, John (eds.), *Nationalism in the Age of the French Revolution* (London: The Hambledon Press, 1988).

Daskalov, Roumen, "Ideas about, and reaction to modernisation in the Balkans", *East European Quarterly*, Vol. 31, No. 2, 1997.

De Rossanet, Bertrand, *Peacemaking and peacekeeping in Yugoslavia* (The Hague: Kluwer Law International, 1996).

Dean, Jonathan, *Ending Europe's Wars* (New York: A Twentieth Century Fund Book, 1994).

Der Derian, James, *On Diplomacy* (Oxford: Basil Blackwell Ltd, 1987).

Der Derian, James and Shapiro, Michael, J. (eds.), *International/Intertextual Relations* (New York, Lexington Books, 1989).

Der Derian, James, *Antidiplomacy: spies, terror, speed, and war* (Cambridge: Blackwell, 1992).

Der Derian, James, *International Theory: Critical Investigations* (Basingstoke: Macmillan Press, 1995).

Derrida, Jacques, *Writing and difference* (London: Routledge, 1995).

Dizdar, Srebren, "A Development and Perspectives of Teacher Education in Bosnia and Herzegovina", Sarajevo, Federal Ministry of Education, Science, Culture and Sports, June, 1998.

Djilas, Milovan, *Tito The Story from Inside* (London: Weidenfeld and Nicolson, 1981).

Doornbos, Martin and Kaviraj, Sudipta (eds.), *Dynamics of State Formation* (London: Sage Publications, 1997).

Doty, Roxanne, Lynn, "Immigration and national identity: constructing the nation", *Review of International Studies*, Vol. 22, 1996.

Dunn, John (ed.), *Contemporary Crisis of the Nation State* (Oxford: Blackwell Press, 1995).

Dunn-Chase, Christopher, "The National State as an Agent of Modernity", *Problems of Communism*, Jan.-Apr. 1992.

Eagleton, Terry, *Literary theory* (UK: Blackwell Publishers, 1996).

Eastby, John, *Functionalism and Interdependence* (New York: University Press of America, 1985).

Edkins, Jenny, Persram, Nalini and Pin-Fat, Veronique (eds.), *Sovereignty and Subjectivity* (London: Lynne Rienner Publishers, 1999).

Erikson, Erik, H., *Identity and the Life Cycle, Psychological Issues* (Bloomington, Indiana: Indiana University Press, 1959).

European Commission External Relations DGIA, "Repairing, reconstructing, reconnecting", Belgium, July, 1998.

European Community Humanitarian Office, "The European Commission's Humanitarian Action in Bosnia and Herzegovina 1998-1999", Sarajevo, 1999.

Evans, Peter, Rueschemeyer, Dietrich and Skocpol, Theda, *Bringing the State Back In* (Cambridge: Cambridge University Press, 1985).

Federico, Joseph, *Confronting Modernity* (Columbia: Camden House, 1992).

Fine, John V.A. and Donia, Robert, J., *Bosnia and Hercegovina: A tradition betrayed* (London: Hurst and Company, 1994).

Finer, Samuel, E., "State-building, state boundaries and border control", *Social Science Information*, Vol. 13, 1974.

Foster, Hal (ed.), *The anti-aesthetic: Essays on Postmodern Culture* (Port Townsend, Wash.: Bay Press, 1983).

Foucault, Michel, *The History of Sexuality, Vol. 1* (Harmondsworth: Penguin, 1979).

Foucault, Michel (Paul Rabinaw (ed.)), *The Foucault Reader* (New York: Pantheon Books, 1984).

Freud, S., *New Introductory Lectures on Psychoanalysis, Lecture 31: The Anatomy of the Mental Personality* (New York: Norton, 1933).

Fukuyama, Francis, *The end of history and the last man* (London: Hamilton Press, 1992).

Gellner, Ernest, *Nationalism* (London: Weidenfeld and Nicolson, 1997).

George, Jim, "International Relations and the Search for Thinking Space: Another View of the Third Debate", *International Studies Quarterly*, 33, 1989.

George, Jim, *Discourses of Global Politics: A Critical (Re)Introduction to International Relations* (Boulder, Colorado: Lynne Rienner Publishers, 1994).

George, Jim, "Realist Ethics, International Relations, and Post modernism: Thinking Beyond the Egoism-Anarchy Thematic", *Millennium*, Vol. 24, No. 2, 1995.

Giddens, Anthony, *The Consequences of Modernity* (California: Stanford University Press, 1990).

Gills, John, R. (ed.), *Commemorations. The Politics of National Identity* (Princeton: Princeton University Press, 1994).

Gramsci, Antonio, *Selections from the Prison Notebooks* (London: Lawrence and Wishart, 1971).

Groom, A.J.R. and Taylor, P., *Frameworks for International co-operation* (London: Pinter Publishers, 1990).

Guehenno, Jean-Marie, *The End of the Nation State* (Minneapolis: University of Minnesota Press, 1995).

Gustavsson, Sverker and Lewin, Leif (eds.), *The Future of the Nation State* (London: Routledge, 1996).

Guzzini, S., *Realism in International Relations and International Political Economy: The Continuing Story of Death Foretold* (New York: Routledge, 1998).

Habermas, Jurgen, *The Philosophical Discourse of Modernity: Twelve Lectures* (Cambridge: Polity Press, 1987).

Halliday, F., *Rethinking International Relations* (Basingstoke: Press, 1994).

Hashi, Iraj, "The Disintegration of Yugoslavia: Regional Disparities and the Nationalities Question", *Capital and Class*, No. 48, 1992.

Hegel, Georg, Wilhelm, Friedrich, *The philosophy of history* (New York: Dover Publications, 1956).

Holbrooke, Richard, *To End A War: From Sarajevo to Dayton and Beyond* (New York: Random House, 1998).

Holbrooke, Richard, "In the Balkans be sure to carry on for the long haul", *International Herald Tribune*, Sept. 15, 1999.

Holm, Hans-Henrik and Srensen, Georg, *Whose world order? Uneven globalisation and the end of the Cold War* (Hans-Boulder: Westview Press, 1995).

Holsti, K.J., *International Politics: a framework for analysis* (New York: Prentice Hall, 1995).

Hume, David, *A Treatise of Human Nature* (London: Fontana Press, 1972).

Independent Bureau for Humanitarian Issues, Human Development Report Bosnia and Herzegovina 1998, Sarajevo, UNDP publication, 1999.

International Crisis Group report, "Changing the Logic of Bosnian Politics: Discussion Paper on Electoral Reform", Sarajevo, 10 March, 1998.

International Crisis Group report, "Doing Democracy a Disservice: 1998 Elections in Bosnia and Herzegovina", Sarajevo, 9 September, 1998.

International Crisis Group report, "State of the Balkans", Sarajevo, 4 November, 1998.

International Crisis Group report, "To Build a Peace: Recommendations for the Madrid Peace Implementation Council Meeting", Sarajevo, 15 December, 1998.

International Crisis Group report, "Breaking the Mould: Electoral Reform in Bosnia and Herzegovina", Sarajevo, Report No. 56, 4 March, 1999.

International Crisis Group report, "Bosnia's municipal Elections 2000: Winners and Losers", Sarajevo, 27 April, 2000.

Jelavich, Barbara, *History of the Balkans* (Cambridge: Cambridge University Press, 1983).

Jelavich, Charles and Jelavich, Barbara, *The Balkans in Transition* (Berkeley: University of California Press, 1963).

Jelavich, Charles and Jelavich, Barbara, *The Establishment of the Balkan National States, 1804-1920* (Seattle: University of Washington Press, 1977).

Kant Immanual, *Perpetual Peace and Other Essays* (trans. Humphrey, Ted, Indianapolis: Hackett Publishing Company, Inc, 1983).

Kantorowicz, Ernst. H., *The King's two Bodies: A study in medieval political theology* (New Jersey: Princeton University Press, 1957).

Keane, Rory, "Dialogue among Civilisations: Creating the institutional framework", 10th International conference, Institute for Political and International Studies, Tehran, January 24-25, 2000.

Keane, Rory, "A new vision for Europe: A challenge to the nation state", Institute on Western Europe, 17th Annual Graduate Student Conference, Columbia University, March 30-April 1, 2000.

Kearney, Richard, *Post nationalist Ireland: politics, literature, philosophy* (New York: Routledge, 1996).

Keohane, Robert and Nye, Joseph, *Power and Interdependence* (Glenview, Illinois: Scott, Foreman and Company, 1989).

Klare, Michael, T. and Thomas, Daniel, C., *World Security, Trends and challenges at century's end* (New York: St. Martin's Press, 1991).

Kratochwil, F., "Of Systems, Boundaries, and Territoriality: An Inquiry into the Formation of the State System", *World Politics*, 1986.

Kratochwil, F., "Systems, Boundaries and Territoriality", *A Quarterly Journal of International Relations*, Vol. XXXIX, No. 1, Oct, 1996.

Lacan, Jacques, *Ecrits: a selection* (translation by Alan Sheridan, New York: W.W. Norton and Company, 1977).

Lacan, Jacques, *The Four Fundamental concepts of psycho-analysis* (Harmondsworth: Penguin Books, 1977).

Lapid, Y. and Kratochwil, F. (eds.), *The Return of Culture and Identity in IR Theory* (London: Lynne Rienner Publishers, 1996).

Lerner, Max (ed.), *The Prince and the Discourses* (trans. Ricci, Luigi, New York: Modern Library, 1950).

Llobere, Josep, R., *The God of Modernity: The Development of Nationalism in Western Europe* (Oxford: Berg Publishers, 1994).

Locke, John, *Political Writings* (Harmondsworth: Penguin Books, 1993).

Luard, Evan, *Basic Texts in International Relations* (Basingstoke: Macmillan Press, 1992).

Lynn-Jones, Sean, M. and Miller, Steven, E. (eds.), *Global Dangers-Changing Dimensions of International Security* (Cambridge, Mass.: M.I.T. Press, 1995).

Lyotard, J.F., *The Postmodern Condition: A Report of Knowledge* (Minneapolis: University of Minneapolis Press, 1984).

Mach, John, "Nationalism and the Self", *Psychohistory Review*, Vol. 11, 1983.

Magee, Bryan, *Popper* (London: Fontana Press, 1985).

Malcolm, Noel, *Bosnia A Short History* (Basingstoke: Macmillan, 1994).

Mangold, Peter, *National Security and International Relations* (London: Routledge, 1990).

Manuel, Frank, E., *The New World of Henri St. Simon* (Indiana: University of Notre Dame Press, 1963).

Marcussen, Henrik, Secher, "NGO's, the State and Civil Society", *Review of African Political Economy*, No. 69, 1996.

Matthew, XVI, *Good News Bible* (London: Collins, 1979).

McCelland, J.S., *A History of Western Political Thought* (London: Routledge, 1996).

McDonald, Lee, Cameron, *Western political theory from its origin to the present* (New York: Harcourt, Brace and World, Inc, 1968).

McSweeney, Bill, *Security, Identity and Interests, A sociology of International Relations* (Cambridge: Cambridge University Press, 1999).

Meyer, John, W., "World Society and the Nation State", *American Journal of Sociology*, July, 1997.

Milosevic, B., "Political Parties", *Yugoslav Life newspaper* (Published by Tanjug News Agency) March, 1990.

Mitchell, W.J.T. (eds.), *The Politics of Interpretation* (London: The University of Chicago Press, 1983).

Mitrany, David, *The Functional Theory of Politics* (London: Martin Robertson & Company Ltd, 1975).

Morgan, Edmund, S., *Inventing the People* (London: W.W. Norton and Company, 1988).

Morgenthau, Hans, *Politics Among Nations* (New York: McGraw-Hill, 1985).

Moss, Jeremy (ed.), *The Later Foucault* (London: Sage Publications, 1998).

Mulheir, Georgette and O' Brien, Tracey, "Private pain, public action: Violence against women in war and peace", *Centre for Peace and Development Studies*, University of Limerick, Ireland, 1999.

Nana-Sinkam, S.C., "From Relief and Humanitarian Assistance to Socio-Economic Sustainability: Rehabilitation, Reconstruction and Development with Transformation as the Ultimate Solution", *International Journal of Refugee Law Special Issue*, Oxford University Press, 1995.

New York Times, "Exuding Confidence, Serbian Nationalists Act as If War for Bosnia is Won", May 23, 1993.

Nietzsche, F., *On the Genealogy of Morals* (trans. W. Kaufmann, New York: Vintage Books, 1967).

Northedge, F. S., *The League of Nations: Its life and times 1920-1946* (Leicester: Leicester University Press, 1988).

Nye, J., "Neo-Realism and Neo-Liberalism", *World Politics*, XL (2), 1988.

Office of the High Representative Website, "New York Declaration, New York, 15 Nov. 1999" (http://www.ohr.int/nyd/en-19991115-ahtml)

Office of the Human Rights Ombudsperson for Bosnia and Herzegovina, Third Annual Report, May 1998, April 1999.

Official Gazette of Bosnia and Herzegovina, Year II, No. 15, Provisional Election Commission Rules and Regulations, OSCE publication, Sarajevo, August, 1998.

Official OSCE Website, "Women can do it seminars support women in politics", November 23, 1999
(http://www.oscebih.org/pressrelease/november1999/23-11-women.htm)

OHR Official Document, "The Dayton Peace Accord", 1995.

OHR Official Document, The Constitution of Bosnia and Herzegovina, 1995.

OHR Official Document, Bosnia and Herzegovina Essential Texts (2nd revised and updated edition), January, 1998.

OHR Official Document, "Reinforcing Peace in Bosnia and Herzegovina: The Way Ahead", Annex to the Madrid Declaration of the Implementation Council, Madrid, 16 December, 1998.

OHR Official Document, Brcko Arbitration Final Award 5 March, 1999 (http;//194.215.227.4/docu/d990305d.htm).

OHR Official Document, "Brcko Novosti", Novosti br.14, July, 1999.

OHR Official Document, "Statute of the Brcko district of Bosnia and Herzegovina", 7 December, 1999.

Onuf, N.G. "Sovereignty: Outline of a Conceptual History", *Alternatives* 16, 1991.

Pavlowitch, Stevan, *Yugoslavia* (London: Ernest Ben Limited, 1971).

Pelczynski, Z.A. (ed.), *Hegel's Political Philosophy: Problems and Perspectives* (Cambridge: Cambridge University Press, 1991).

Peterson, Spike, V. *Gendered States-Feminist (Re)Vision of International Relations Theory* (London: Lynne Rienner Publishers, 1992).

Pfetsch, Frank R. (ed.), *International Relations and Pan-Europe* (Heidelberg: LIT Verlag, 1993).

Pick, Otto and Critchley, Julian, *Collective Security* (Basingstoke: Macmillan publishers, 1974).

Plato, *Republic* (trans. Davies, John Llewelyn and Vaughan, David James, London Wordsworth Editions Limited, 1997).

Pogge, Thomas, W., "Cosmopolitanism and Sovereignty", *Ethics* 103, October, 1992.

Powers, Gerard, F., "Religion, conflict and prospects for reconciliation in Bosnia, Croatia and Yugoslavia", *Journal of International Affairs*, Vol. 50, No. 1, Summer, 1996.

Pridham, Geoffrey, *Building Democracy? The international dimension of democratisation in Eastern Europe* (Leicester: Leicester University Press, 1997).

Refugee Trust Ireland, "Social and health profile of the most vulnerable elderly people in Hrasnom, Ilidza, Grbavica and Mostar", September, 1997.

Reiss, Hans (ed.), *Kant-Political Writings* (Cambridge: Cambridge University Press, 1970).

Rice, Timothy, *May it fill your soul* (Chicago: University of Chicago Press, 1994).

Roberts, Adam and Kingsbury, Benedict (eds.), *United Nations, Divided World* (Cambridge: Clarendon Press, 1988).

Rorty, Richard, *Contingency, Irony, and Change* (Cambridge: Cambridge University Press, 1989).

Rousseau, Jean-Jacques, *Du contrat social. The social contract and Discourses* (London: Dent, 1973).

Ruggie, J.G., "Territoriality and beyond: problematizing modernity in international relations", *International Organization*, Vol. 47, No. 1, 1993.

Ruggie, J.G., *Constructing the World Polity* (London, Routledge, 1998).

Said, Edward, "Nationalism, Colonialism and Literature: Yeats and Decolonisation", *A Field Day Pamphlet*, Number 15, 1988.

Schierup, Carl-Ulrik, *Migration, Socialism and the International Division of Labour* (Aldershot: Avebury, 1990).

Scott, Boulder and London, *Modern History* (London: Westview, 1984).

Scott, P.H., *The Union of Scotland and England* (Edinburgh: Chambers Ltd, 1979).

Shue, Henry, *Basic Rights Subsistence, Affluence and US Foreign Policy* (Princeton: Princeton University Press, 1980).

Silber, Laura and Little, Allan, *The Death of Yugoslavia* (Marmondsworth: Penguin Press, 1995).

Simons, Marlise, "Between Migrants and Spain: The Sea That Kills", *The New York Times*, March 30th, 2000.

Singleton, Fred, *A Short History of the Yugoslav Peoples* (New York: Cambridge University Press, 1985).

Sjolander, Claire Turenne and Cox, Wayne, S. (eds.), *Beyond Positivism Critical Reflections on International Relations* (London: Lynne Rienner Publishers, 1994).

Smith, S., "Paradigm dominance in international relations: The development of international relations as a social science", *Journal of International Studies*, Vol. 16, No. 2, 1987.

Smith, Booth, and Zalewski, *International Theory: Positivism and Beyond* (Cambridge: Cambridge University Press, 1996).

Snyder, Louis (ed.), *The dynamics of nationalism* (New Jersey: D. Van Nostrand Company, Inc, 1964).

Sorensen, G., "An Analysis of Contemporary Statehood: Consequences for conflict and co-operation", *Review of International Studies*, 23, 1997.

Soyal, Yasemin, Nuhoglu, *Limits of Citizens* (London: The University of Chicago Press, 1994).

Spiro, Peter, J., "New Global Communities: Nongovernmental Organisations in International Decision-Making Institutions", *The Washington Quarterly*, Winter 18:1, 1995.

Stanley, Winters and Held, J. (eds.), "Intellectual and Social Developments in the Habsburg Empire from Maria Theresa to World War 1", Boulder: Colo, *East European Quarterly*, 1975.

Strayer, Joseph, R., *On the Medieval Origins of the Modern State* (Princeton: Princeton University Press, 1970).

Taylor, Paul and Groom, A.J.R., *International Organisation* (London: Frances Pinter Ltd, 1978).

Teich, Mikulas and Porter, Roy (eds.), *The National Question in Europe in Historical Context* (Cambridge: Cambridge University Press, 1993).

The ICVA Directory of humanitarian and development agencies in Bosnia and Herzegovina, April 1999.

Tipton, Leon, C., *Nationalism in the Middle Ages* (Melbourne, Florida: Krieger Publishing, 1972).

Tomasevich, Jozo, *Peasants, Politics and Economic Change in Yugoslavia* (Stanford: Stanford University Press, 1955).

Toulmin, Stephen, *Cosmopolis* (Chicago: Chicago University Press, 1990).

UNHCR, "Information Notes", No.6/98-November December, 1998.

UNHCR, "Information Notes", No. 5/98-September October, 1998.

UNHCR, "Statistics Package", Sarajevo Operations Unit, I July, 1999.

Vasques, J.A., *Classics of International Relations* (New Jersey: Prentice Hall, 1990).

Vincent, R.J., "Edmund Burke and the Theory of International Relations", *Review of International Studies*, 10, 1984.

Viroli, Maurizio, *From Politics to Reason of State* (Cambridge: Cambridge University Press, 1992).

Visker, Rudi, *Michel Foucault Genealogy as Critique* (London: Verso, 1995).

Vuckovic, Gojko, "Failure of socialist self-management to create a viable nation-state and disintegration of the Yugoslav administrative state and state institutions", *East European Quarterly*, Boulder: Fall, Vol. 32, Issue 3, 1998.

Vulliamy, Ed, *Seasons in Hell: Understanding Bosnia's War* (London: Simon and Schuster, 1994).

Waever, Ole, "Identity, Integration and Security", *Journal of International Affairs*, 2, 1995.

Waever, Ole, Buzan, Barry, Kelstrup, Morten and Lemaitre, Pierre (eds.), *Identity, Migration and the New Security Agenda in Europe* (London: Pinter Publishers Ltd, 1993).

Walker, R.B.J., *The Concept of Security and International Relations theory* (University of California: Institute of Global Conflict and Co-operation, 1987).

Walker, R.B.J., "Security, Sovereignty, and the Challenge of World Politics", *Alternatives* XV, 1990.

Walker, R.B.J., *Inside/Outside: International Relations as Political Theory* (Cambridge: Cambridge University Press, 1993).

Walsh, Jennifer, M., *Edmund Burke and International Relations* (Oxford: St. Martin's Press, 1995).

Waltz, K., *Man, the State and War* (New York: Columbia University Press, 1959).

Waltz, K., *Theory of International Politics* (New York: Random House, 1979).

Weber, Cynthia, *Simulating Sovereignty* (Cambridge: Cambridge University Press, 1995).

Weiss, Thomas. G. (ed.), *Collective Security in a Changing World* (London: Lynne Rienner Publishers, 1993).

West, Rebecca, *Black Lamb and Grey Falcon* (Basingstoke: Macmillan London Limited, 1955).

Whitaker Raymond, "Homecoming Serbs bring new heartache to Sarajevo", *The Independent on Sunday*, July 16, 2000.

Wilkinson, Ray, "A Decisive Year", *Refugees*, Vol. 1, No. 114, 1999.

Williams, Howard, *Kant's Political Philosophy* (Cardiff: University of Wales Press, 1992).

Williams, John, *Legitimacy in International Relations and the Rise and Fall of Yugoslavia* (Basingstoke: Macmillan Press, 1998).

Williams, John, "Toleration, Territorial Borders and International Society", Paper for British International Studies Association Annual Conference, University of Sussex, 1998.

Williams, John, "The Ethics of Borders and the Borders of Ethics: International Society and rights and duties of special beneficence", Paper presented to the Department of International Relations, University of St. Andrews and the ECPR Standing Group on IR/ISA Third Pan-European Conference on International Relations, 1999.

Wilson, Thomas, M. and Donnan, Hastings, *Border Identities* (Cambridge: Cambridge University Press, 1998).

Woodward, Susan, *Tragedy, Chaos and Dissolution after the Cold War* (Washington: The Brookings Institute, 1995).

Wright, Martin, *The System of States* (Leicester: Leicester University Press, 1977).

Young, C. (ed.), *The Rising Tide of Cultural Pluralism* (Wisconsin: The University of Wisconsin Press, 1993).

Youngs, Gillian, *International relations in a global age* (Cambridge: Polity Press, 1999).

Yugoslav Life newspaper, "More Stable Development", Volume XXIX, No. 10-12, October-December, 1984.

Zalewski, Marysia and Parpart, Jane (eds.), *The "Man" Question in International Relations* (Boulder, Colo.: Oxford: Westview Press, 1998).

Zizek, Slavoj, *For they know not what they do. Enjoyment as a political factor* (London: Verso Press, 1991).

Zizek, Slavoj, *Tarrying with the Negative-Kant, Hegel and the critique of Ideology* (Durham: Duke University Press, 1993).

Zolo, Danilo, *Cosmopolis* (Cambridge: Polity Press, 1997).

Appendix 1

Interviews conducted in Bosnia and Herzegovina and Serbia

Date	Name of Interviewee	Organisation/ Location	Position held
3-7-99	Mr. Morris Power	Office of the High Representative, Sarajevo	Return Reconstruction Task Force (RRTF)
4-7-99	Mr. James Fergusson	Office of the High Representative, Sarajevo	Public Affairs Division
7-7-99	Mr. sc. Dzemal Subasic	Ministry for Social Policy, Displaced Persons and Refugees, Sarajevo	Chief Advisor to Minister.
7-7-99	Mrs. Sanela Paripovic	Ombudsperson for Bosnia and Herzegovina, Sarajevo	Deputy Ombudsperson
9-7-99	Mr. Claude Kieffer	Office of the High Representative, Sarajevo	Chief Education Officer
13-7-99	Mr. Peter Krale	European Community Monitoring Mission (ECMM)	Head of Bosnian desk
15-7-99	Miss Fidelma Donlon	Office of the High Representative, Mostar	Human Rights Officer
17-7-99	Mr. Andrew MacGregor	Organisation for Security and Cooperation in Europe, Sarajevo	Human Rights Officer – Education Portfolio
18-7-99	Mr. Zdravko Ljubas	International Federation of Red Cross and Red Cross Crescent Societies, Sarajevo	Information Assistant
18-7-99	Mr. Joakim Robertsson	European Community Monitoring Mission (ECMM), Sarajevo	Special Advisor to Head of Mission
19-7-99	Mr. Christopher Harlands	Office of the High Representative, Sarajevo	Human Rights Officer

22-7-99	Miss Danelli Cavine	European Community Humanitarian Office (ECHO), Sarajevo	Information Officer
26-7-99	Mr. Olivier Mouquet	United Nations High commission for Refugees, Mostar	Liaison Officer
28-7-99	Mr. Kristof Gosztonyi	Office of the High Representative, Mostar	Return Reconstruction Task Force (RRTF)
31-7-99	Mrs. Renale Herrmanns	Organisation for Security and Cooperation in Europe, Mostar	Regional Spokesperson
31-7-99	Mr. Thomas Peyker	European Union, Mostar	European Commission Representative
5-8-99	Mr. Veselin Jovanovic	Refugee Trust Ireland, Sarajevo,	Reconstruction and Return Program Officer
7-8-99	Mrs. Sauelie Golubouid	Organisation for Security and Cooperation in Europe, Banja Luka	Priority Return Officer
8-8-99	Miss. Zlatica Gruhonjic	Organisation for Security and Cooperation in Europe, Banja Luka	Regional Election Officer
10-8-99	Mr. Pasi Poysari	Office of the High Representative, Banja Luka	Political Advisor
11-8-99	Mr. Denyft Ronny	European Community Monitoring Mission, Banja Luka	Head of Regional Mission
12-8-99	Mr. Jose Maria Aranaz	Office of the High Representative, Banja Luka	Human Rights and Legal Officer
16-8-99	Mr. Shin Umezu	United Nations Mission to Bosnia and Herzegovina, Brcko	Civil Affairs Officer
17-8-99	Mr. Mike Austin	Office of the High Representative, Brcko	Political Officer
17-8-99	Mr. Stuart Paucher	Office of the High Representative, Brcko	Returns Officer
18-8-99	Mr. Jonathan Stonestreet	Organisation for Security and Cooperation in Europe, Brcko	International Election Officer
19-8-99	Mr. Lionel Meny	European Community Monitoring Mission, Brcko	Team Leader – Field Officer
25-8-99	Mr. Gavin W. Hood	Independent Bureau for Humanitarian Issues (IBHI), Sarajevo	Consultant
27-8-99	Mr. Michael Cox	United States Agency for International Development (USAID), Sarajevo	Democracy Specialist
28-8-99	Mr. Josip Polic	European Bank for Reconstruction and Development (EBRD), Sarajevo	Monitoring Officer
29-8-99	Mrs. Wendy Rappeport	United Nations High Commission for Refugees, Sarajevo	Public Information Officer

1-9-99	Miss. Lejla Somun	Independent Bureau for Humanitarian Issues (IBHI), Sarajevo	Resident Director
2-9-99	Dr. Desmund Maurer	University of Sarajevo, Sarajevo	Faculty of Philosophy, Department of English
2-9-99	Mr. Niall McCann	International Crisis Group, Sarajevo	Justice Program Manager
4-9-99	Miss Tricia C. Marlar	Organisation for Security and Cooperation in Europe, Sarajevo	Deputy Director for Public Information
5-9-99	Mr. Kare Vollan	Organisation for Security and Cooperation in Europe, Sarajevo	Deputy Head of Mission for Elections
6-9-99	Mr. Alex Finnen	Organisation for Security and Cooperation in Europe, Sarajevo	Director General of Elections
7-9-99	Mrs. Claudia Schafer	Organisation for Security and Cooperation in Europe, Sarajevo	Information Officer
16-2-00	Miss Sanela Becirovic	Organisation for Security and Cooperation in Europe, Sarajevo	Deputy Spokesperson for BiH
15-5-00	Mr. Alexander Nitzsche	Organisation for Security and Cooperation in Europe, Sarajevo	Press Officer
4-3-01	Miss Sanela Becirovic	Organisation for Security and Cooperation in Europe, Sarajevo	Deputy Spokesperson for BiH
15-4-01	Mr. Obrad Savic	Belgrade Circle	Editor-in-Chief
30-4-01	Mr. Paul Rowland	National Democratic Institute for International Affairs	Program Director-Serbia
2-5-01	Dr. Jelica Kurjak	Institute of International Politics and Economy, Serbia	Senior Researcher
4-5-01	Mr. Yannich du Pont	Academic Training Association, Kosovo	President
14-5-01	Mr. Slobodan Markovich	Belgrade Open School	Programme Co-Ordinator

Appendix 2

The governmental structure of BiH as outlined in annex IV
of the Dayton Peace Accord.

Peace Implementation Council (PIC)

Office of the High Representative (OHR)

1. Constitutional Court of Bosnia and Herzegovina

2. Presidency of Bosnia and Herzegovina (BiH)

(Troika - Elected)

3. Council of Ministers (Selected)

4. Bicameral parliamentary assembly

BiH House of representatives   BiH House of people

(Elected)   (Selected)

Federation Bosnia and Herzegovina (FBiH)	**Republika Srpska (RS)**
5. Federation Presidency (Elected)	R.S. Presidency (Elected)

6. Federation BiH Bicameral Assembly   R.S. National

Assembly

FBiH House of Representatives - House of Peoples

(Elected)   (Selected)   (Elected)

7. Federation BiH Cantonal Assemblies (10 Elected)   (None)

8. Municipal Assemblies   Municipal Assemblies

(Elected)   (Elected)

9. Voters Federation BiH   Voters R.S.

Bosnia and Herzegovina, Political Structure Chart, prepared by W.G.

Robinson Q.C. Senior Council, OSCE, 1 October 1996.

Appendix 3

Brcko Arbitration Rulings (14 February 1997)

No.	External agency	Role
1	OHR Supervisor	Promulgation of binding regulations and orders
2	OHR, OSCE, UNHCR, SFOR EBRD, IMF, and others	Advisory Council
3	SFOR and IPTF	Democratic policing
4	UNHCR, Commission for DP's and Refugees, and other agencies	Organisation of return
5	Deputy High Representative and OSCE	Organisation of elections and issues of regulations
6	International development agencies	Economic revitalisation
7	Public and private investors	Revive Sava river port
8	International customs monitors	Customs controls
9	State of BiH and Republic of Croatia	Customs and border crossings

Chandler, David, *Bosnia, Faking Democracy after Dayton*, London: Pluto Press, 1999, p.85.

Index